Warman's

Little Golden Books

FIELD GUIDE

Steve Santi

Values and Identification

©2005 Steve Santi

Published by

kp books
An Imprint of F+W Publications

700 East State Street • Iola, WI 54990-0001
715-445-2214 • 888-457-2873

Our toll-free number to place an order or obtain a free catalog is
(800) 258-0929.

Library of Congress Catalog Number: 2005922627

ISBN: 0-89689-265-4

Designed by Wendy Wendt

Edited by Mary Sieber

Printed in the United States of America

Table of Contents

The History of Little Golden Books

Western Publishing Company, Inc., one of the largest printers of children's books in the world, had its beginning in the basement of 618 State Street in Racine, Wisconsin.

Edward Henry Wadewitz, the 30-year-old son of German immigrants, had been working two jobs—one at a paint store and the other for West Side Printing Company—while taking bookkeeping classes at night. When the owner of the printing company was unable to pay Wadewitz his wages, he offered to sell Wadewitz the business. With dreams of owning his own business, Wadewitz, with $2,504 (some of it borrowed from his brother, Al), purchased the West Side Printing Company in 1907.

Wadewitz knew that if the printing company were to make it, he would need someone with more knowledge than he had. Roy A. Spencer, a printer with the Racine Journal Company, was one of the first people Wadewitz hired.

Western Publishing Company started in 1907 in this basement print shop. "Pioneer employees" were (from left) Roy A. Spencer, Catherine Bongarts Rutledge, E. H. Wadewitz, W. R. Wadewitz, and William Bell. The shop consisted of not much more than two battered presses, a few fonts of worn type, and a hand-powered cutting machine.

West Side Printing Company, with four employees, showed sales of $5,000 at the end of its first year. In 1908, with commercial job sales increasing, the company hired more employees. That year it also left a $10-a-month rental building and moved into a larger one and purchased a new automatic cutting machine and three new presses.

In 1910, after the purchase of the company's first lithographic press, the name was changed to Western Printing and Lithographing Co.

A major sign of Western Publishing Company's growth was the 1929 move to the new main plant in Racine, Wisconsin.

Less than four years later, the company moved into an even larger space—the basement of the Dr. Clarendon I. Shoop Building located at State and Wisconsin Avenue in Racine. Dr. Shoop was famous for bottled medications and tonics. Western Printing and Lithographing Co. had become so successful that when Dr. Shoop retired in 1914, the company took over all six floors of the Shoop Building.

By its seventh year, sales had topped $127,000 and two new departments were formed: electrotyping and engraving. The company also purchased a new 28-inch by 42-inch offset press.

Wadewitz was approached by the Hamming-Whitman Publishing Company of Chicago to print its line of children's books.

What Wadewitz did not foresee was that Hamming-Whitman would soon be going out of business. Unable to pay its bills, Hamming-Whitman left Western with thousands of books in its warehouse and in production.

Trying to cut its losses, Wadewitz entered Western into the retail book market for the first time. It proved so successful that the remaining Hamming-Whitman books were liquidated.

After acquiring Hamming-Whitman on Feb. 9, 1916, Western formed a subsidiary corporation called Whitman Publishing Company. Whitman employed two salesmen the first year and grossed more than $43,500 in children's book sales.

Sam Lowe, who later owned Bonnie Books, joined the Western team in 1916. Lowe sold Western and Whitman on the idea of bringing out a 10-cent children's book in 1918. Disaster almost followed when an employee misread a book order from S.S. Kresge Company, confusing dozens for gross, resulting in too many books being printed. Lowe was able to sell F.W. Woolworth Company and other chains the idea of having children's books on sale all year round. Until that time, stores usually treated children's books as Christmas items.

Toward the end of 1918, Western was outgrowing the Shoop Building, so another one was purchased—named Plant 2—to house the bookbinding and storage departments. In order to print a 6-inch by 9-inch book, Western purchased a 38-inch by 52-inch Potter offset press in 1923. This same year, Western started producing games and puzzles.

With sales of more than $1 million in 1925, Western decided to add another product, playing cards, to its growing line of merchandise. To be able to handle this, Western obtained the Sheffer Playing Card Company and formed another subsidiary corporation, the Western Playing Card Company.

By 1928, Western had built a new, modern, air-conditioned plant on Mound Avenue in Racine, and by 1929, sales were more than $2.4 million. The print run for children's books exceeded $10 million, playing cards $5 million, and games and puzzles $1 million. As a result, the company had to make plans to expand its new building.

In 1929, Western purchased Stationer's Engraving Company of Chicago, a manufacturer of stationery and greeting cards. This was the second operation the company had outside of Racine.

In 1910 West Side Printing Company changed its name to Western Printing & Lithographing Company and moved to the imposing building seen here, which was owned by Dr. Shoop's Laboratories.

Western was able to keep its plant operational during the Depression years (1929-1933) by introducing a couple of new products: The Whitman jigsaw puzzle became very popular during this time of uncertainty, and a new series of books called Big Little Books was marketed. Brought out in 1932, the 10-cent Big Little Books became very popular during the years when people were looking for inexpensive entertainment. The first Big Little Book title was *The Adventures of Dick Tracy*. With this line of books, Western was setting the stage for future inexpensive reading material like comic books and Little Golden Books. People love to copy success, and many publishers started bringing out their own books styled after the Big Little Book.

By the end of 1933, the Depression was coming to a close, Disney's Big Bad Wolf had been beaten by the Three Little Pigs, and Western and Walt Disney signed their first contract, giving Western exclusive rights to Disney's major characters.

Western, seeing a problem in having its plants and offices so far from the rest of the publishing industry, purchased a plant in Poughkeepsie, New York, in 1934. This event marked the beginning of a close relationship with Dell Publishing Company and Simon & Schuster, Inc. Dell Publishing and Western produced Color Comics, which contained many of Western's licensed characters, from 1939 to 1962. *A Children's History* was the first joint effort between Western and Simon & Schuster in 1938.

Western formed the Artists and Writers Guild Inc. in the 1930s to handle the development of new children's books. This company, located on Fifth Avenue in New York City, would later have an immense hand in the conception of Little Golden Books.

Western expanded its operations to the West Coast when it opened an office in Beverly Hills, California, sometime in the early 1940s. Being closer to the movie capital of the world made it a lot easier to do business with the studios that owned the characters the company licensed.

During World War II, Western did its part to help with the war effort. The company had a contract with the U.S. Army Map Service to produce maps for American soldiers in the fields. Along with the maps and other projects it did for the military, Western also manufactured many of its own products that were sent to the soldiers and the Red Cross overseas, such as playing cards and books.

In 1940, Sam Lowe left the company and George Duplaix replaced him as head of the Artists and Writers Guild. While the guild and Simon & Schuster were collaborating on a book about Walt Disney's Bambi, Duplaix came up with the concept of a colorful children's book that would be durable and affordable to more American families than those being printed at that time. In 1941, children's books sold for between $2 and $3—a luxury for a lot of families. With the help of Lucile Olge, also of the guild, Duplaix contacted Albert Leventhal—a vice president and sales manager at Simon & Schuster—and Leon Shimkin, also of Simon & Schuster, with his idea.

The group decided on 12 titles to be released at the same time. Each title would have 42 pages, 28 printed in two-color and 14 printed in four-color. The book's binding was designed after a side-staple binding being done in Sweden. These books were to be called Little Golden Books.

The group originally discussed a 50-cent price for Little Golden Books, but Western did not want to compete with the other 50-cent books already on the market. The group did some more figuring and found that if it printed 50,000 copies of each book instead of 25,000, the books could be sold for 25 cents each. In September 1942, the first 12 titles were printed and released to stores in October.

Little Golden Books, with their colorful, bright pages, were designed to be handled by children and were inexpensive enough that children could read or handle their books whenever they wanted. With these qualities and many more, the books became very popular with parents, but not with librarians in these early years, who felt these books did not contain the quality of literature a child should be reading. They did not consider that a book a child could handle was better than one stored out of reach on a shelf, or that an affordable book was better than not owning one at all, but this attitude has mellowed quite a bit since the 1940s.

The first ad to announce Little Golden Books was published in the Sept. 19, 1942, edition of *Publisher's Weekly*. The ad listed the types of stories and the artists creating the first 12 books. The ad stated the books measured 8-1/4 inches by 6-1/4 inches and contained 44 pages—30 pages in black and white and 14 in full color. Whether it was because of the war, getting the price down to a quarter, or a printing error in the ad, the books were released with 42 pages, not 44.

The First 12 Little Golden Books

1   *Three Little Kittens*
2   *Bedtime Stories*
3   *The Alphabet From A to Z*

4   *Mother Goose*
5   *Prayers for Children*
6   *The Little Red Hen*
7   *Nursery Songs*
8   *The Poky Little Puppy*
9   *The Golden Book of Fairy Tales*
10   *Baby's Book*
11   *The Animals of Farmer Jones*
12   *This Little Piggy*

Within five months, 1.5 million copies of the books had been printed and they were in their third printing. They became so popular with children that by the end of 1945, most of the first 12 books had been printed seven times. Simon & Schuster, Inc. published Little Golden Books, while the Artists and Writers Guild produced them, and Western Printing and Lithographing printed them.

When the books were first released, they were sold mainly in book and department stores. From there, they moved into variety, toy, and drug stores, and finally in the late 1940s, to something new called the supermarket. Often, parents did not mind paying a quarter for a book, so, for the first time, a quality children's book was made available to children who normally couldn't have afforded one.

During World War II, there was a paper shortage in the United States. To help ease this shortage, in 1943 the War Production Board put restrictions on paper use. As a result, retailers were receiving only one of every 10 books they ordered. Some Little Golden Book titles were being printed with fewer than the original 42 pages. In some cases, the size of the book was also reduced slightly. Books that had been reduced to compensate for the paper shortage stated on the copyright page "First Printing this edition."

Most of the first 35 titles were released with blue bindings. Books that have this binding were published with dust jackets. Book No. 35, The Happy Family, was the last book published with the blue binding.

The purchase of U.S. Savings Stamps was mentioned on the back inside flap of the dust jackets of these early books. One of the characters of each of the books was also used to talk to the child about purchasing these stamps.

The following are some of these shorts:

THREE LITTLE KITTENS

They found their mittens and they rushed out to say,
"Oh! Mother dear, see here, see here our mittens we have found."
"What! Found your mittens, you good little kittens!
I'll get you all War Stamps today!"
So, you be good kittens, hold onto your mittens, save your pennies the War Stamp way!

BEDTIME STORIES

One day Chicken Little strutted through the woods.
Behind her strutted Henny Penny and Ducky Lucky and Goosey Loosey. On the way they met Turkey Lurkey.
"Where are you going?" asked Turkey Lurkey.

"We are all going to buy War Savings Stamps, just as we do every week!"
So Turkey Lurkey joined them and they all hurried off to buy War Savings Stamps. And so should you!

FROM A TO Z

A is for the airplanes which Jimmy's War Stamps buy.
B is for the Bond he'll get to keep them in the sky.
C is for children who save a bit each day.
D is for the dimes they save that help the U.S.A.
You can buy Stamps every week, like Jim. Soon you'll be buying a Bond, like him.

MOTHER GOOSE

There was an old woman who lived in a shoe.
She had so many children,
She knew just what to do.
She gave them some broth without any bread,
Bought them all War Stamps
And sent them to bed.
Soon she was able to buy them a War Bond.
If you buy War Stamps with your pennies, soon you can buy a Bond too.

PRAYERS FOR CHILDREN

Today our country, which has given us so much, needs our help. It asks all of us, children and grown-ups alike, to put our savings into War Stamps and Bonds.
These Bonds will help to buy the ships and tanks and planes and guns our country needs to win the war quickly.

Then, too, we will get back all the money we invest, and more, later on.
Surely we will all want to buy War Stamps or Bonds every week to help our country!

THE LITTLE RED HEN

This year the Little Red Hen has a Victory Garden. She has extra food to sell to the duck, the goose, the cat and the pig who will not grow their own.
With the pennies she saves, she buys War Savings Stamps every week. Soon she will have enough stamps to buy a War Bond.
If you buy War Stamps every week, you will soon be able to buy a Bond too.

NURSERY SONGS

Mary buys War Savings Stamps, Savings Stamps, Savings Stamps,
Mary buys War Savings Stamps to help the U.S.A.
Soon she's going to have a Bond, Have a bond, Have a Bond,
Soon She's going to have a Bond.
Why not start yours today?

THE POKY LITTLE PUPPY

The poky little puppy sat near the bottom of the hill, looking hard at something on the ground in front of him.
"What is he looking at?" the four little puppies asked one another. And down they went to see.
There was a War Savings Stamp lying on the grass. And

the poky little puppy hurried home faster than he had ever run before, to paste the stamp in his War Stamp Book. All the five little puppies buy War Stamps every week.
So should you.

THE GOLDEN BOOK OF FAIRY TALES

While the wicked Old Giant was asleep, Jack tucked the magic hen under his arm, and fled down the beanstalk to his home.
Every day the hen laid a golden egg, and Jack sold the gold to buy a War Savings Bond, which is much more valuable.
Even if you don't have a magic hen, your pennies will buy War Savings Stamps and soon you will be able to buy a Bond too!

BABY'S BOOK

Where is Tommy?
Here he is.
He has a new War Stamp.
Soon he will buy a War Bond.
Do you buy War Stamps every week like Tommy?
Of course you do!

THE ANIMALS OF FARMER JONES

All the animals are hungry. But Farmer Jones has gone to town. He is buying War Savings Stamps. He buys War Savings Stamps every week. You should buy War Stamps every week, too.
Soon you will be able to buy a War Savings Bond.

THIS LITTLE PIGGY AND OTHER COUNTING RHYMES

This little piggy goes to market.
What do you think he'll buy?
He's buying some War Savings Stamps.
So do I.
This little piggy cried, "Wee, wee, wee, Boo! hoo! hoo!
I have no War Savings Stamps." Is that you?

THE GOLDEN BOOK OF BIRDS

Robin Redbreast's beak is high and he is singing proudly,
he has just bought War Stamps for the whole Robin
Family.
If you save your pennies and buy War Stamps, you will
want to sing, too.

NURSERY TALES

You remember how the kind old shoemaker and his wife
made tiny shoes and tiny jackets and trousers and hats
for the good little elves who helped them. (If you don't
remember, you can read about them in this very book.)
Well, one night the elves came back. They crept into the
shop and left a gift on the shoemaker's workbench. What
do you suppose that gift was? It was a War Savings Stamp
Book half filled with War Savings Stamps. These days, a
War Savings Stamp is the best gift of all!

A DAY IN THE JUNGLE

All the animals were on their way to visit the mouse. The
story had spread that he had something really worth

seeing, and all were anxious to find out what this tiny animal could possibly have that was worth looking at. But they all gasped when he showed it to them—a brand new twenty-five-dollar War Bond!

"How," growled the lion, "did you manage to do that?" "I just kept buying War Stamps," said the mouse, "and pretty soon I had enough for a bond. It was quite simple." If a mouse can do it, can't you, too?

THE LIVELY LITTLE RABBIT

The red squirrel was very wise, told all the animals that buying War Stamps was a very fine thing to do. All the rabbits hurried off to take his advice. And who do you think was the first in line? The lively little rabbit, of course. Then all the other little rabbits, and the squirrel, and the owl, and yes, even the weasels, bought their War Stamps. And so should you!

THE GOLDEN BOOK OF FLOWERS

If Miss Petunia, the Rose, the shy Violet, the naughty Daisy, the Water Lily, the Goldenrod and all our other flower friends could come right out of this book to speak to you today they would all say: "BUY MORE WAR STAMPS"

HANSEL AND GRETEL

Hansel and Gretel have learned how to provide for the future. Each week they buy War Savings Stamps, and soon they are going to buy a Bond. It's a good way for you to save, too.

MY FIRST BOOK OF BIBLE STORIES

Just as Joseph asked the Egyptians to set aside part of their crop to provide for the years to come, so your Government is asking you to use part of your money to buy War Savings Stamps.

Once the paper shortage was over, the books were again printed in their original 42 pages. Back orders that had piled up during the shortage began to be filled, and the company found itself with thousands of new customers.

Sales of Little Golden Books were doing so well that in 1944, Simon & Schuster decided to create a new division headed by George Duplaix, called Sandpiper Press. Duplaix hired Dorothy Bennett—who was formerly employed as the assistant curator at the Museum of Natural History—as the general editor. She was responsible for many of the subjects used in Little Golden Books through the mid-1950s, and she authored numerous books, including The *Giant Golden Book Encyclopedia*. Bennett fought very hard to keep television and movies out of Little Golden Books; she felt the quality and context of the books would be weakened. She hated to see the book *J. Fred Muggs* printed and thought it poetic justice when the monkey bit the host and the television show was taken off the air. Bennett wanted the books to teach children something of the world they lived in, whether it was history, geography, science, or the experiences a child has while growing up.

In the 1940s, Little Golden Books, dealing with good little boys and girls and their experiences of everyday life, were approved by Mary Reed, Ph.D., assistant professor of education at the Teacher's College, Columbia University. Reed went on to supervise the subject matter of Little Golden Books until 1961.

Walt Disney Little Golden Books have been published since 1944, but it wasn't until 1947 that new stories were published quite regularly and have been ever since. The first three books of the Disney series were published under Walt Disney's Little Library before being changed to A Little Golden Book. The first three stories originally came with dust jackets.

Doctor Dan, the Bandage Man, Little Golden Book No. 111, was released in January 1951. The first printing of the book was 1,750,000, the largest first printing on any Little Golden Book to date. Six Johnson & Johnson Band

Aids® were glued down the right side of the title page. Later, girls were given equal time with *Nurse Nancy*. As the *Doctor Dan* stories changed, so did the style of the Band-Aids included with the book; later there were circus and stars and stripes varieties.

In 1952, on the tenth anniversary of Little Golden Books, approximately 182,615,000 Little Golden Books had been sold. *The Night Before Christmas* alone sold more than four million copies! In their eleventh year, almost 300 million Little Golden Books had been sold. More than half of the titles printed by 1954 had sold more than a million copies each. Little Golden Books were now available almost everywhere in the world except the Soviet Union. Little Golden Books, including *The Poky Little Puppy*—which had the distinction of being labeled a capitalistic story—were not allowed to be sold in the Soviet Union.

May 1, 1954, was the release date of *Little Lulu and Her Magic Tricks*, with a first printing of 2,250,000. The book had a small package of Kleenex® tissues in its front cover and directions for making tissue toys. Such an extensive advertising and promotional campaign was launched for the book that it was even shown on the "Arthur Godfrey Show" in the month of the book's release.

Quite a few of the titles in the 1950s showed that children were starting to spend a lot of time in front of their television sets. By the mid-1950s, children's TV shows and westerns were top sellers in Little Golden Books, while in the early 1960s, the books were about Saturday morning cartoon shows. From 1965 to the early 1970s, though, Little Golden Books dropped TV and went back to printing original stories about growing up.

Activity Series

In 1955, Little Golden Books were released in the activity series, which ran until 1961. This series consisted of books with learning wheels, stamps, paper dolls, paper models, paint and coloring books, and even a calendar. This was not a new idea for Little Golden Books; back in the early 1950s, the company brought out books with masks, puzzles, stencils, decals, tape, tissue, and, as previously mentioned, Band-Aids.

In 1958, Little Golden Books were released in *A Giant Little Golden Book*. Most of these contained three Little Golden Books of the same subject in one volume.

In 1958, Western Publishing and Lithographing Co., Inc. and Pocket Books Inc. became joint publishers, and the company name then became Golden Press, Inc. But in 1960, Western Printing and

Lithographing became Western Publishing Company, Inc. and Pocket Books' interest in Golden Press was acquired in 1964.

In 1959, a series of Little Golden Books called a *Ding Dong School Book*, written by Dr. Frances R. Horwich, was published by Golden Press. "Ding Dong School" was a children's television show in the 1950s hosted by Miss Frances.

Boxed puzzles, made from cover art of Little Golden Books, were produced in the early 1950s. The boxes were a little smaller than the original books. There were four series. Value ranges from $35-$85.

The first series consisted of:

The Lively Little Rabbit
The Five Little Firemen
The Jolly Barnyard
The Poky Little Puppy
The Shy Little Kitten
Tootle

The second series consisted of:

The Alphabet from A to Z
A Year on the Farm
Johnny's Machines
The Wonderful House
The Marvelous Merry-Go-Round
Dr. Dan the Bandage Man

The third series consisted of:

Busy Timmy

Little Black Sambo
When You Were a Baby
Little Yip Yip and His Bark
The Happy Man and His Dump Truck
A Day At The Playground

The fourth series consisted of:

Katy the Kitten
How Big
Brave Cowboy Bill
Little Golden
A Day at the Beach
Train to Timbuctoo

There was also a release of tray puzzles by Playskool®. These puzzles came in a box of four, and each set featured a certain subject. The pictures were of Little Golden Book covers or inside art. Each puzzle in the set had a different number of pieces for ages 4 to 8. Value per set is $25-$40.

Puzzle Sets:

80-1 Animal Babies
80-2 Ways to Travel
80-3 Horses and Colts
80-4 Fairy Stories
80-5 Life of a Cowboy
80-6 Indian Pals
80-7 Farms and Farming
80-8 Children and Religion

80-9 Funny Animals
80-10 Workers We Know
80-11 Dogs and Puppies
80-12 Children in Action

The Golden Hours Library was produced in 1967. This consisted of a box shaped like a clock, with moving hands, that contained 12 Little Golden Books in miniature. Value is $45.

The books were:

How to Tell Time
Heidi
The Big Little Book
Old MacDonald Had A Farm
Four Little Kittens
Rumpelstiltskin
Hop Little Kangaroo
Four Puppies
The Littlest Raccoon
Tommy's Camping Adventure
Colors Are Nice
Little Cottontail

In 1972, Golden produced an 11-1/2-inch by 14-inch four-tray puzzle boxed set. Each set contained four puzzles about a Little Golden Book, with the condensed story printed on the box's inside top flap. Two titles were *The Poky Little Puppy* and *The Lively Little Rabbit. Scuffy the Tugboat* Game was also produced in this series.

In 1974, Little Golden Books were published in the Eager Reader series. These books were printed with large type for beginning readers.

In 1977, Western Publishing developed a series called A Little Golden Game for children ages 5 to 8, which were games based on Little Golden Books. The boxed cover was a duplicate of the Little Golden Book that the game depicted. Four books that were produced as games were *Old MacDonald Had a Farm, Jack and the Beanstalk, The Three Little Pigs,* and *The Little Red Caboose.*

Little Golden Books have been printed in more than 42 countries. Most of these countries release the same titles as the United States, although a few have had original titles of their own.

In 1982, Little Golden Books were 40 years old and more than 800 million books had been sold. On Nov. 20, 1986, the one billionth Little Golden Book was printed in the United States, *The Poky Little Puppy.* Australia celebrated the printing of its 200 millionth Little Golden Book in February 1988.

The Little Golden Book Numbering System

Little Golden Books were originally numbered 1 through 600, starting with No. 1, *The Three Little Kittens*, in 1942, and ending with 600, *Susan in the Driver's Seat*. But just because they were numbered does not mean they were published in sequential order. For instance, book 205 was published two years before 204, and some numbers never had a title. In 1971, new releases began to be numbered by going back to 105. Later, 102 through 104 were redone. One possibility for the renumbering not continuing past 600 could be that 615 through 630 had already been given to My First Golden Learning Library in 1965. This was a series of books, illustrated by William Dugan and written by Jane Werner Watson, with different colored foil spines and letters of the alphabet broken down in a dictionary-type format.

The books of the 1970s had no chronological order of publishing—they were published in the 100, 200, 300, and 500 numbers. The only similarity I have noticed in these different numbers is that the two books redone in the 500s were science fiction.

In 1979, Western changed its numbering again to the new numbering system; for example, with 101-42, 1 indicates assortment, 01 indicates category, and -42 indicates position in category. If you are trying to collect by book numbers, I recommend that you collect the first edition and forget the numbers because the categories' subject matter may change each year.

The year 1997 brought another change to the numbering system: The book numbers became five numbers followed by a dash and followed by one or two numbers. Most of these begin with a 9, but there are a few beginning with an 8.

In 2004 numbers are no longer present on the books. As a reference number for these books, I list the third set of numbers in the ISBN. For example, with ISBN 0-7364-**2095**-9, I list 2095. This will be a four- or five-digit number.

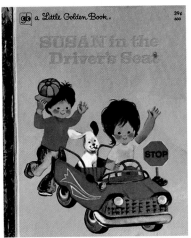

Susan in the Driver's Seat *is book #600.*

How to Determine Editions

1. **1942-1946:** Edition number will be found on the first or second page of the book. Most of these books have blue spines and dust jackets.

2. **1947-1970:** Look on the last page of the book in the lower right-hand corner by the spine. There will be a letter that will correspond with the edition. For example A=first, Z=26th, AA=27th.

3. **1971-1991:** On the bottom of one of the first two pages you will see something like ABCDEFGHIJKLM. The first letter to the far left is the edition. A= first

4. **1991-2001:** These books, besides having the copyright date, will also have a printing date in Roman numerals. If a book from this period does not have a Roman numeral date, it is a first printing and the number was left off by mistake. If the letter "A" precedes the Roman numeral, the book is a first edition. If an "R" precedes the Roman numeral, then the book is a revised edition. If there is no letter preceding the Roman numeral, the numerals themselves state when the book was printed, and there is no way to determine the edition.

For those of you not familiar with Roman numerals, "MCMXCI" is 1991. When reading Roman numerals, you subtract the number on the left from the one on the right when the one on the left is smaller. M =1,000, C=100, X=10, IX=9 (or 10 minus 1), VIII=8, VII=7, VI=6, V=5, IV=4 (or 5 minus 1), III=3, II=2, I=1. With the number "MCMXCI," you have "M"=1000, "CM"=900 (or 1000 minus 100), "XC"=90 (or 100 minus 10), "I"=1 for 1000 + 900 + 90 + 1 = 1991.

5. **2001-Present:** Sometime in 2001, the Roman numerals were dropped for the more standard method of determining book editions. In this method, the last number to the right of a row of numbers is the edition/printing.

10 9 8 7 6 5 4 3 2 1 is a first edition. Most first editions will also state "First Edition."

10 9 8 7 6 5 4 3 is a third edition/printing.

6. There are cases where the edition marking was forgotten. If none of the above examples can be used, there is a good chance your book is a first edition.

In this case I recommend trying to use other means to determine if your book is a first edition. For books that have numbered titles on the back cover, you can take the last book number listed on the back of the book, look up its copyright date in this guide, and compare it with the copyright of the book you are not sure of. This way of checking is also a good way to find out approximately when a book was printed, give or take a year.

The Changing Price of Little Golden Books

The price of Little Golden Books has changed quite a bit since 1942, when they sold for 25 cents each. Twenty years later, the price increased to 29 cents. This was followed by 39 cents in 1968, 40 cents in 1974, 59 cents in 1977, 69 cents in 1979, 89 cents in 1982, and 99 cents in 1986. Books printed today no longer have a price printed on the front cover. Starting sometime in 2004, cover prices of $2.50 to $2.99 can be found on the bottom left corner of the inside front cover and the bottom left corner of the back cover.

Counting Rhymes

How to Use This Guide

This field guide lists book titles alphabetically. There are around 700 books pictured. Values given are for first editions in very fine or better condition.

If your title is not listed in the picture section, check the listing in the back of the book for more titles and values. In the picture section, I have tried to show only pictures of first editions or first cover printings of a book's title. When a title with the same author and artist was printed with a different number, I have listed the other numbers and values. I have done this for numbers 1 to 600, Disney titles D1 to D139, and the Activity titles. I do not list multiple numbers on the later books because these numbers are actually codes. I have tried to give the first printing codes for these later books. If you need to know more of the dash codes used on the later titles, many of them are mentioned in my other book, *Collecting Little Golden Books*. If you are looking up a later title and it's not a first edition, and the number/code is not listed in this guide, then treat it as you would any other reprint.

Reprints: How Much to Deduct From the Listed Values

Many of you would love to have a magic formula to deduct from the prices listed to determine the value of reprints. Unfortunately, because some titles had many reprints and others maybe only one, there is no magic formula.

A second edition of a title with only two printings would be worth more than a second edition of a title with 10 reprints. If you know the book had many reprints (i.e., *Little Red Riding Hood, Bedtime Stories*, and *The Poky Little Puppy*), a reprint will not be worth much, unless it's a 42-page edition with the original pages or if a significant change had been made to the book. Reprints of books that have fewer pages than the original will be worth quite a bit less than an edition with the original number of pages. If the book had only one reprint, the reprint could sell for close to the value of the original book.

If you want to know how many reprints a book had, you're out of luck. Most of this information has been lost over the years. As you search through stacks of Little Golden Books, you will notice the stories with many reprints.

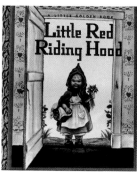

Little Red Riding Hood *has been reprinted numerous times.*

Condition Value Percentages

100%   Mint: No marks of any kind on book. Should look like it just came off the store shelf.

80%-90%   Very Fine: This is a book that would be mint condition except for very few scuff marks.

75% **Fine:** Clean, tight book. May have some light erasable pencil marks. Name may be written on inside cover in space provide. A little of the cover luster may be gone. Overall condition of the book should indicate that the book was read but was well cared for.

60%-70% **Very Good**: Above average condition. Well taken care of book with no major flaws.

50%   Good: Average. May have some light soiling or chipping on front cover. No tears or scrapes on the cover. The inside pages may have small creases or folded corners, could have small tears no more than a quarter-inch long. No tape. Some of the spine cover may be missing or chipping. The book is well read but still in complete condition.

25%   Fair: The spine is getting loose. The cover is soiled. There is no crayon scribbling or ink to distract from any part of the book. There may be some tape on pages. The book is well-read and not taken care of.

0%-10% **Poor**: Damaged. Crayon, ink on pages, missing or chewed pages, missing activities. The book probably looks like it just came out of the trash.

The First 12 Little Golden Books

#1 Three Little Kittens (see listing on page 437)

#2 Bedtime Stories (see listing on page 86)

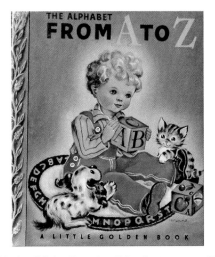

#3 The Alphabet From A to Z (see listing on page 58)

#4 Mother Goose (see listing on page 302)

#5 Prayers for Children (see listing on page 367)

#6 The Little Red Hen (see listing on page 274)

#7 Nursery Songs (see listing on page 337)

#8 The Poky Little Puppy (see listing on page 363)

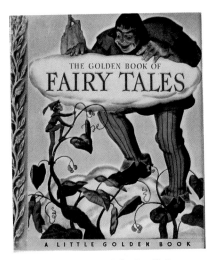

#9 The Golden Book of Fairy Tales (see listing on page 198)

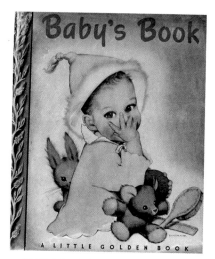

#10 Baby's Book (see listing on page 75)

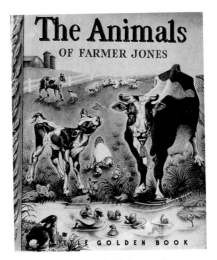

#11 The Animals of Farmer Jones
(see listing on page 65)

#12 This Little Piggy (see listing on page 432)

Little Golden Books

Alphabetical By Title
(Listed with copyright dates, book numbers and current first edition values in very fine or better condition.)

1 2 3 Juggle With Me!
©1970
594 ....$6

5 Pennies to Spend

©1955

238 ....$20

A B C Around the House

©1957

A 18 ....$30

A 44 ....$25

Without wheel $6

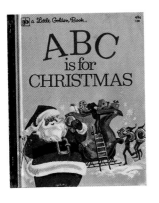

A B C Is For Christmas
©1974

108 ....$6

A B C Rhymes
©1964

543 ....$6

About the Seashore

©1957

284 .... $7

Adventures of Buster Hood, The

©1991

111-72.....................$4

Aladdin

©1959

371..........................$13

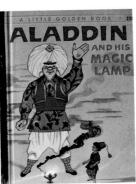

Albert's Zoo—A Stencil Book

©1951

112 .... $80

Without stencils...................... $10

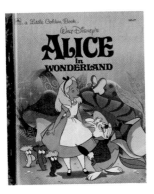

Alice In Wonderland

©1991

105-77.......................$3

Alice In Wonderland Finds the Garden of Live Flowers

©1951

D20..........................$16

Alice In Wonderland Meets the White Rabbit

©1951

D19...$16

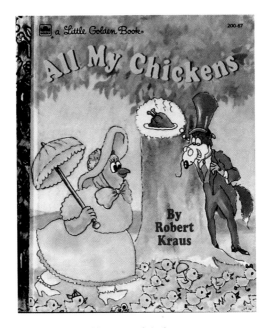

All My Chickens

©1993

200-67.....................................$5

Alphabet From A to Z, The

©1942

3 ....$40

First edition with dust jacket .... $50-$200

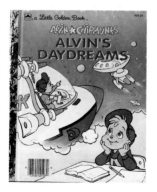

Alvin's Daydreams

©1990

107-73.......................$5

Amanda's First Day of School
©1985
204-56.........................$4

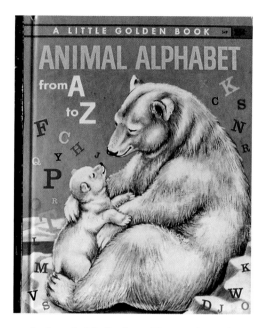

Animal Alphabet From A to Z

©1958

349 .... $10

Animal Babies

©1947

39 ....$16

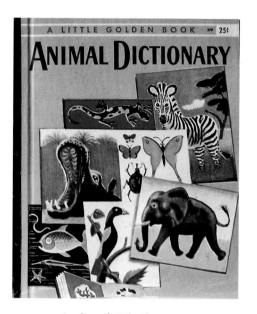

Animal Dictionary

©1960

Animal Friends

©1953

167 .... $12
560 .... $5

Animal Quiz

©1960

396 ....$6

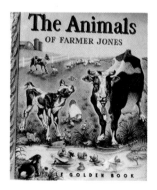

Animals of Farmer Jones, The

©1942

11 ....$40
First edition with dust
jacket .... $50-$200

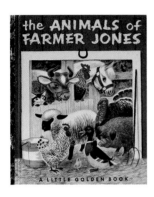

Animals of Farmer Jones, The

©1953

211 ....$10

282 ....$8

Animals On the Farm

©1968

573 ....$4

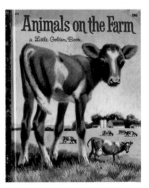

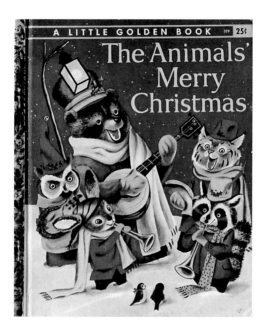

Animals' Merry Christmas, The

©1958

329 ....$16

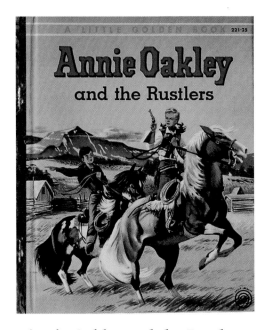

Annie Oakley and the Rustlers
©1955
221 ....$20

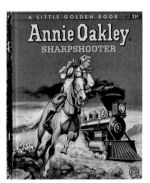

**Annie Oakley
Sharpshooter**

©1956

275 .... $20

Aren't You Glad

©1962

489 .... $6

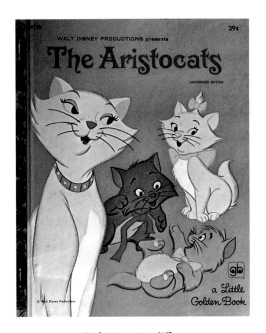

Aristocats, The

©1970

D122..$15

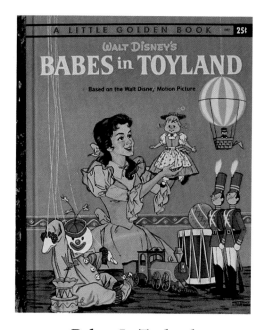

Babes In Toyland

©1961

D97..$13

Baby Dear

©1962

466 ....$18

Baby Farm Animals

©1958

333 .... $7

464 .... $6

Baby Listens

©1960

383 .... $15

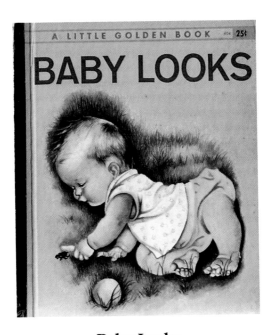

Baby Looks

©1960

404 ....$17

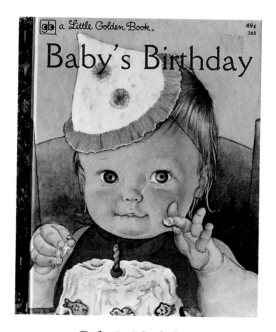

Baby's Birthday

©1972

365 ....$10

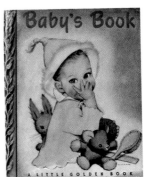

Baby's Book

©1942

10 .... $75

First edition with dust
jacket ....$75-$300

Baby's Christmas

©1959

460-08 .... $4

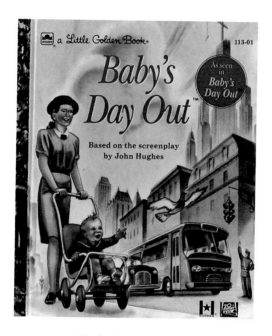

Baby's Day Out

©1994

113-01..$5

Baby's First Book
©1959
358 ....$7

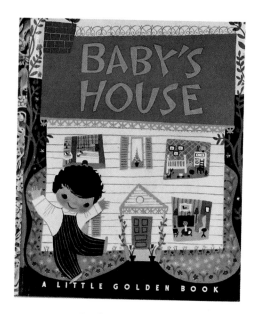

Baby's House

©1950

80...$20
"B" edition with complete puzzle $150

Baby's Mother Goose

©1957

303 ....$8
422 ....$6

Bambi

©1948

D7..$18

D90..$4

Bamm-Bamm

©1963

540 ....$22

Barbie

©1974

125 ....$9

**Barbie—A
Picnic Surprise**

©1990

107-70......................$5

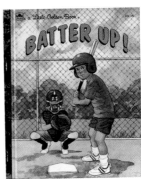

Batter Up!
©1991

211-68......................$5

Beach Day
©1988

208-57......................$4

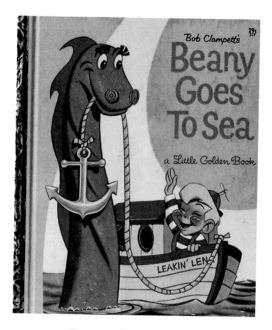

Beany Goes to Sea

©1963

537 ....$22

Beauty and the Beast

©1991

104-65......................$3

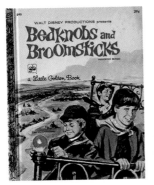

Bedknobs and Broomsticks

©1971

D93...........................$8

Bedtime Stories

©1942

2 ....$40

239 ....$7

364 ....$6

538 ....$5

First edition with dust jacket ....$50-$200

Ben and Me

©1954

D37.......................$16

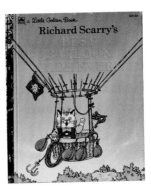

Best Balloon Ride Ever!

©1994

208-68......................$3

Best Friends

©1983

209-46......................$5

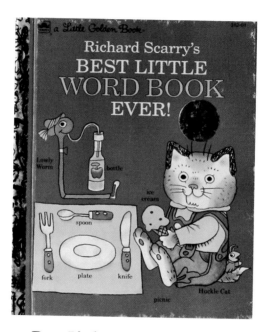

Best Little Word Book Ever!

©1992

312-01.......................................$3

Bettina the Ballerina

©1991

211-69.....................................$60

Bialosky's Special Picnic
©1985
204-55......................$5

Bible Stories From the Old Testament
©1977
153 ....$6

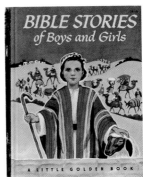

Bible Stories of Boys and Girls

©1953

174 .... $8

Big Bird Brings Spring to Sesame Street

©1985

108-57 .... $5

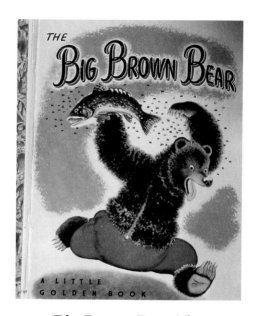

Big Brown Bear, The

©1947

89 .... $25

335 .... $8

**Big Enough
Helper, The**
©1978
152 .... $6

**Big Little Book,
The**
©1962
482 .... $7

Big Red

©1962

D102.......................$12

Birds of All Kinds

©1959

380 ....$6

**Bisketts In
Double Trouble**

©1985

107-47 .... $3

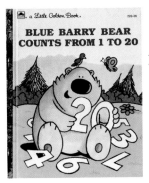

**Blue Barry Bear
Counts From
1 to 20**

©1991

203-59 .... $3

Blue Book of Fairy Tales, The

©1959

374 ....$15

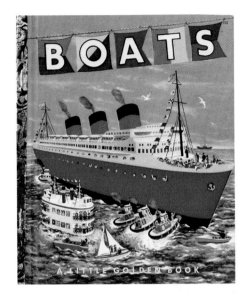

Boats

©1951

125	$8
339	$6
501	$5

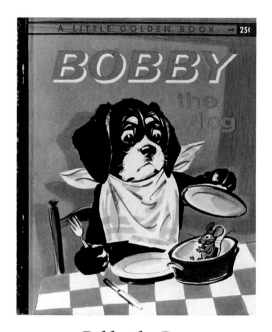

Bobby the Dog

©1961

440 ....$20

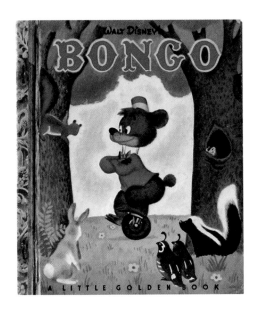

Bongo

©1948

D9..$18
D62..$10

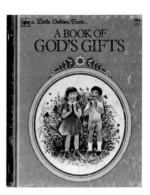

Book of God's Gifts, A

©1972

112 .... $6

Bow Wow! Meow! A First Book of Sounds

©1963

523 .... $6

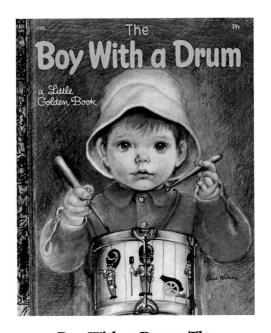

Boy With a Drum, The

©1969

588 ....$15

Bozo Finds a Friend
©1962
485 .... $10

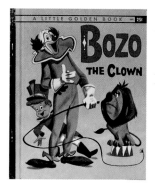

Bozo the Clown
©1961
446 .... $10

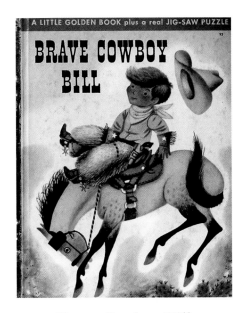

Brave Cowboy Bill

©1950

93 ....$125
Without puzzle $20

Brave Eagle

©1957

294 ....$17

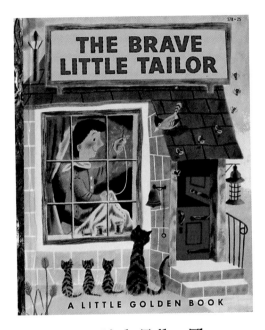

Brave Little Tailor, The

©1953

178 .... $10

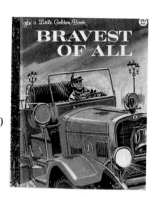

Bravest of All

©1973

402 .... $10

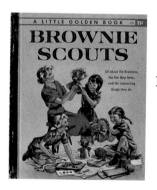

Brownie Scouts

©1961

409 .... $17

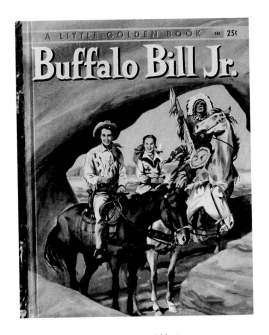

Buffalo Bill Jr.
©1956
254..$20

Bugs Bunny
©1949

72 .... $15

312 .... $6

475 .... $5

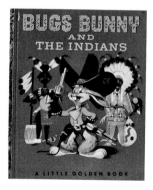

Bugs Bunny
and the Indians
©1951

120 .... $14

430 .... $8

Bugs Bunny and the Pink Flamingos

©1987

110-63.....................$5

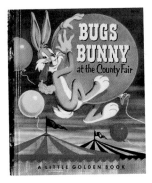

Bugs Bunny At the County Fair

©1954

164 ....$14

Bugs Bunny
Gets a Job
©1952
136 .... $12

Bugs Bunny's
Birthday
©1950
98 .... $14

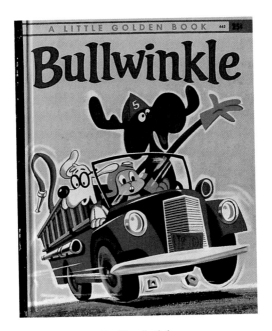

Bullwinkle

©1962

462 ....$18

**Bunnies'
Counting Book,
The**
©1991
203-58.....................$3

Bunny Book
©1951
D111......................$15

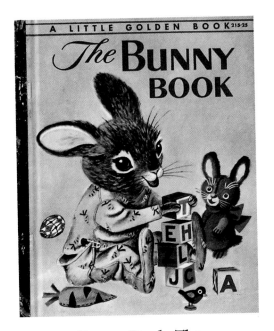

Bunny Book, The

©1955

215 ....$8

Bunny's New Shoes

©1987

204-60......................$4

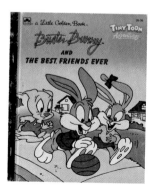

Buster Bunny and the Best Friends Ever

©1991

111-76......................$4

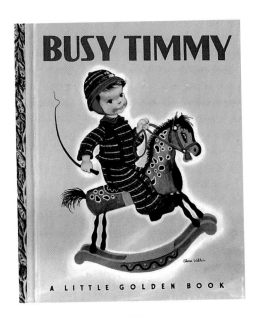

Busy Timmy

©1948

50 ....$35
452 ....$13

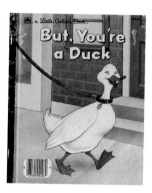

But, You're A Duck
©1990
206-58..................... $3

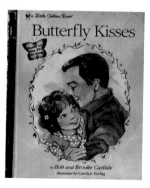

Butterfly Kisses
©1997
98872 .... $2

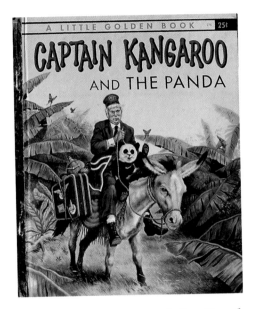

Captain Kangaroo and the Panda

©1951

278 .... $13
421 .... $7

Cars
©1956

251 .... $8

Cars
©1973

566 .... $4

Cat That Climbed the Christmas Tree, The

©1992

458-03.....................$3

Cats

©1976

150 ....$6

Cave Monster, The
©1996
107-52.....................$3

Charlie
©1970
587 ....$7

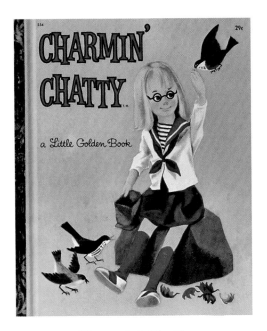

Charmin' Chatty

©1964

554 ....$20

Chelli Tells the Truth
©1997
98822 .... $2

Cheltenham's Party
©1985
201-56 .... $5

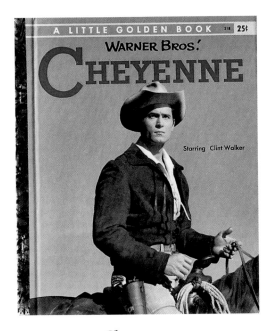

Cheyenne

©1958

318 ....$20

Chicken Little
©1960
413 .... $7

Chicken Little
©1973
524 .... $4

Child's Garden of Verses, A

©1957

289 .... $10

493 .... $7

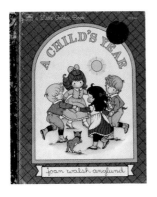

Child's Year, A

©1992

312-06 .... $5

Chip 'n Dale At the Zoo

©1954

D38.........................$17

Chip 'n Dale Rescue Rangers—The Big Cheese Caper

©1991

105-78......................$3

Chip Chip

©1947

28 .... $25

First edition is unstated and lists to book #35 on back cover and dust jacket.

First edition with dust jacket .... $50-$150

Chipmunk's
A B C
©1963

512 ....$7

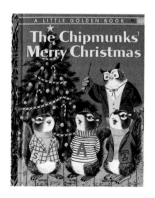

Chipmunks'
Merry
Christmas, The
©1959

375 ....$10

Chitty Chitty Bang Bang

©1968

581 ....$10

**Christmas
A B C, The**
©1962
478 .... $25

**Christmas
Bunny, The**
©1994
450-13 .... $3

Christmas Carols

©1946

26.. $20
595... $4
First edition is unstated and lists to book #34 on back
cover and #36 on dust jacket.
First edition with dust jacket............................$50-$125

Christmas In the Country
©1950

95 .... $25

Christmas Manger
©1953

176 .... $18

Christmas Story, The

©1952

158 ....$15

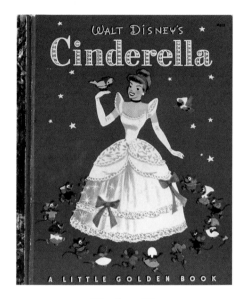

Cinderella

©1950

D13..$16
D59..$10
D114..$10

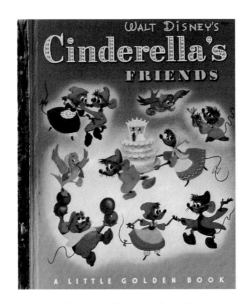

Cinderella's Friends

©1950

D17...$16
D58...$10
D115...$7

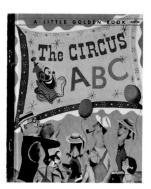

Circus A B C, The

©1955

222 .... $18

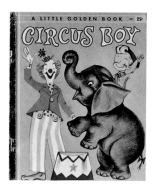

Circus Boy

©1957

290 .... $25

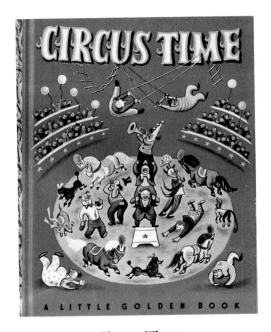

Circus Time

©1948

31 ....$20

Cold-Blooded Penguin, The

©1944

D2..$45

First edition with dust jacket

....$50-$150

Color Kittens, The

©1949

86...$25
436..$10
"B" edition with complete puzzle $125

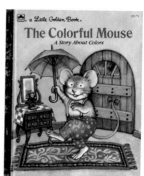

Colorful Mouse, The

©1991

211-71.......................$4

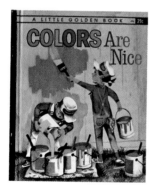

Colors Are Nice

©1962

496 ....$6

Come Play House

©1948

44 ....$35

Corky's Hiccups

©1973

503 ....$6

Count All the Way to Sesame Street

©1985

203-56......................$4

Count to Ten

©1957

A16 .... $35
A43 .... $25
Without wheel $6

Counting
Rhymes
©1946

12 ....$20

With dust
jacket ....$50-$150

Counting
Rhymes
©1947

257 ....$7

Counting Rhymes

©1960

361 ....$6

**Country Mouse
and the City
Mouse, The**

©1961

426 .... $7

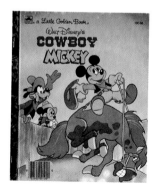

Cowboy Mickey

©1990

100-63 .... $3

**Curious Little
Kitten Around
the House, The**

©1986

206-57 .... $5

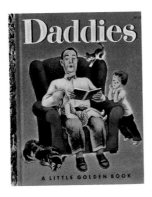

Daddies

©1954

187 .... $20

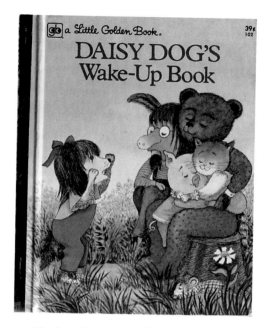

Daisy Dog's Wake-Up Book
©1974
102 ....$25

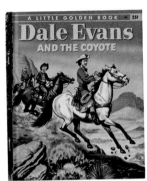

**Dale Evans and
the Coyote**

©1956

253 .... $20

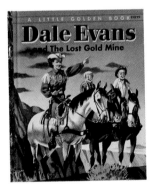

**Dale Evans and
the Lost Gold
Mine**

©1954

213 .... $20

Daniel In the Lions' Den

©1987

311-62......................$5

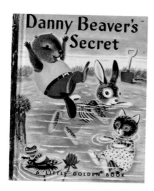

Danny Beaver's Secret

©1953

160 ....$15

Darkwing Duck—The Silly Canine Caper

(Unstated First)

©1992

102-67 .... $3

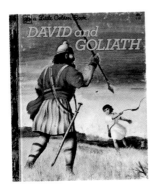

David and Goliath

©1974

110 .... $6

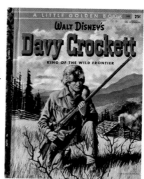

Davy Crockett— King of the Wild Frontier

©1955

D45.........................$16

Davy Crockett's Keelboat Race

©1955

D47.........................$18

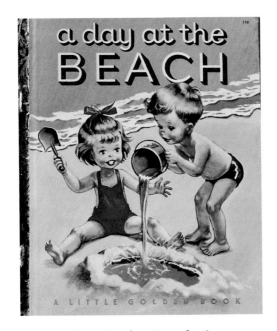

Day At the Beach, A

©1951

110 ....$25

Day At the Playground, A

©1951

119 .... $25

Day At the Zoo, A

©1949

88 .... $14

324 .... $8

Day Snuffy Had the Sniffles, The

©1988

108-59 .... $5

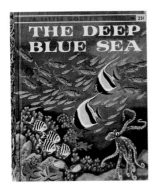

Deep Blue Sea, The

©1958

338 .... $6

**Dennis the
Menace—A
Quiet Afternoon**

©1960

412 .... $10

**Dennis the
Menace Waits
For Santa Claus**

©1961

432 .... $17

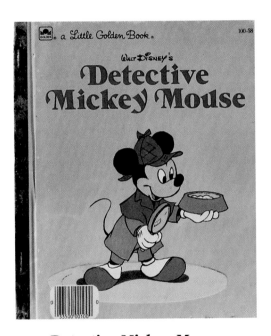

Detective Mickey Mouse

©1985

100-58..$5

Dick Tracy
©1962
497 .... $22

Dinosaurs
©1959
355 .... $6

Disneyland On the Air

©1955

D43..........................$15

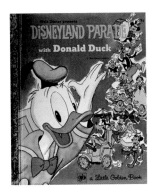

Disneyland Parade

©1971

D123..........................$8

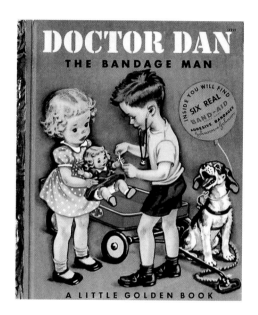

Doctor Dan, the Bandage Man

©1950

111 ....$100

Without Band-Aids $18

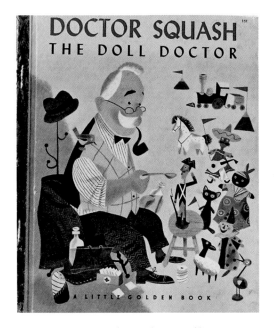

Doctor Squash—The Doll Doctor
©1952

157 ....$20

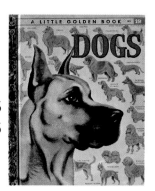

Dogs

©1952

391 .... $6

532 .... $6

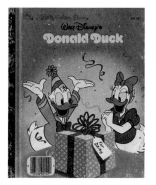

Donald Duck—
Some Ducks
Have All the
Luck

©1987

102-56..................... $5

Donald Duck
and Santa Claus
©1952

D27.........................$16

Donald Duck
and the Biggest
Dog In Town
©1986

102-55......................$5

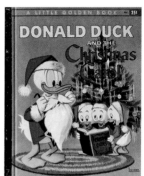

Donald Duck
and the
Christmas Carol
©1960
D84.........................$40

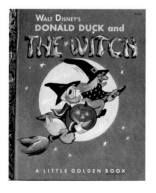

Donald Duck
and the Witch
©1953
D34.........................$20

Donald Duck and the Witch Next Door

©1974

D127..........................$6

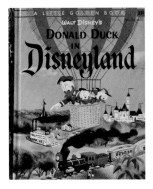

Donald Duck In Disneyland

©1954

D44..........................$16

D92..........................$12

D109........................$10

Donald Duck—Instant Millionaire

©1978

D140.........................$7

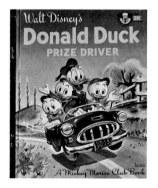

Donald Duck— Prize Driver

©1956

D49.........................$18

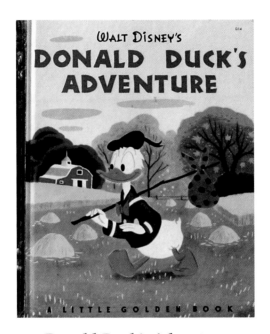

Donald Duck's Adventure

©1950

Donald Duck's Christmas Tree

©1954

D39..........................$16

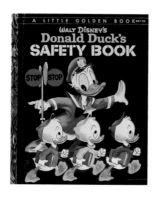

Donald Duck's Safety Book

©1954

D41..........................$20

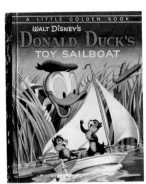

Donald Duck's Toy Sailboat

©1954

D40.........................$16

Donald Duck's Toy Train

©1950

D18.........................$16

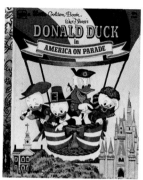

Donald Duck In America On Parade

©1975

D131.........................$9

Donnie and Marie—The Top Secret Project

©1977

160 ....$8

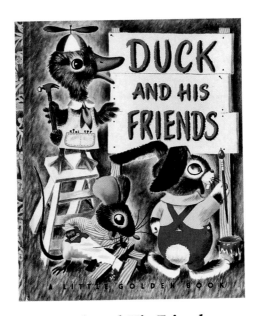

Duck and His Friends

©1949

81..$14
"B" edition with complete puzzle $100

Dumbo

©1947

D3...$45

First edition with dust jacket
.....................................$50-$200

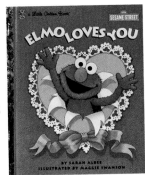

Elmo Loves You
©1997

98846 .... $2

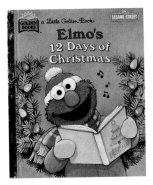

Elmo's 12 Days of Christmas
©1996

98787 .... $3

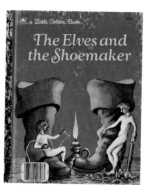

Elves and the Shoemaker, The

©1983

307-61...................... $3

Emperor's New Clothes, The

©1993

207-66...................... $3

Exploring Space
©1958
342 .... $8

**Fairy Princess,
The (Superstar
Barbie)**
©1977
162 .... $7

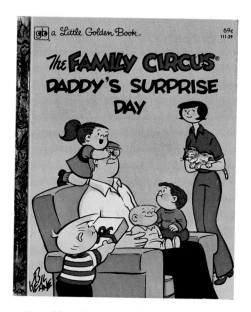

Family Circus, The—Daddy's Surprise Day

©1980

111-29......................................$25

Favorite Nursery Tales

©1973

D125 .... $6

Fire Engines

©1959

382 .... $7

Fire Engines to the Rescue

©1991

306-58......................$3

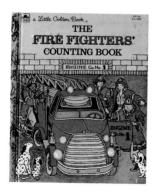

Fire Fighters' Counting Book, The

©1983

203-45......................$5

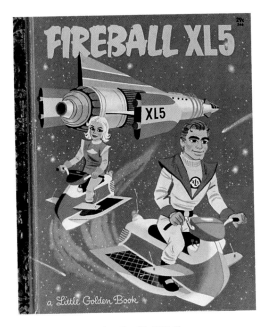

Fireball XL5

©1964

546 ....$27

First Airplane Ride, A

©1986

310-57 .... $3

First Bible Stories

©1954

198 .... $20

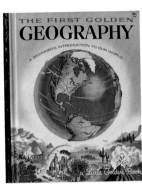

**First Golden
Geography, The**

©1955

534 .... $6

**First Little
Golden Book of
Fairy Tales, The**

©1946

9 .... $20

With dust
jacket .... $50-$100

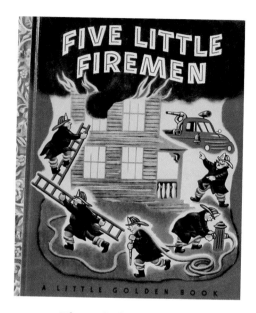

Five Little Firemen

©1948

64 ....$30

301 ....$12

Flintstones, The

©1961

450 .... $20

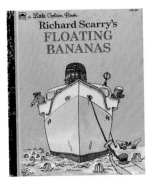

Floating Bananas

©1993

208-65 .... $3

Fly High
©1971
597 .... $7

**Flying
Dinosaurs**
©1990
309-51 .... $4

Flying Is Fun!
©1986
310-53......................$5

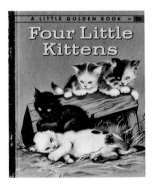

Four Little Kittens
©1957

322 ....$6

530 ....$6

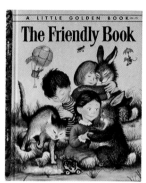

**Friendly Book,
The**
©1954
199 .... $15
592 .... $5

**Frosty the Snow
Man**
©1951
142 .... $15

Fun For Hunkydory

©1963

521 ....$7

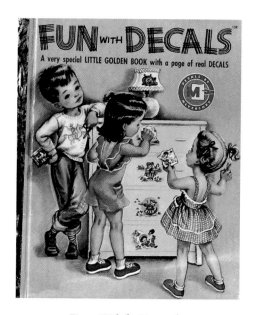

Fun With Decals

©1952

139 ....$125
Without decals..........................$15

Fury
©1957
286 .... $16

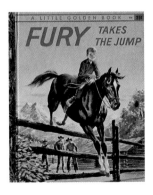

Fury Takes the Jump
©1958
336 .... $15

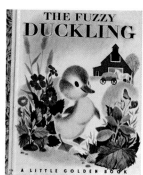

Fuzzy Duckling, The

©1949

78 ....$15

557 ....$6

Gaston and Josephine

©1949

65 ....$30

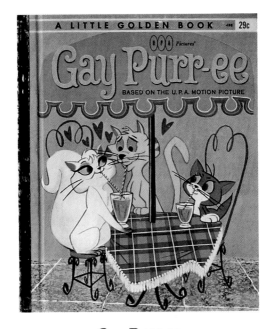

Gay Purr-ee
©1962

488 ....$22

Gene Autry
©1955
230 .... $22

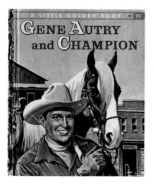

Gene Autry and Champion
©1956
267 .... $22

Georgie Finds A Grandpa

©1954

196 .... $25

Ghost Ship

©1991

104-62 .... $3

**Giant Who
Wanted
Company, The**

©1979

207-4 .... $5

**Giant With the
Three Golden
Hairs, The**

©1955

219 .... $16

Ginger Paper Doll

©1957

A14 ....$90

A32 ....$85

Without clothes and dolls $5

Gingerbread Man, The

©1953

165 .... $11

437 .... $6

Gingerbread Shop, The

©1952

126 .... $20

Ginghams, The—Backward Picnic, The

©1976

148 .... $6

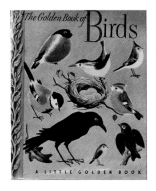

Golden Book of Birds, The

©1943

13 .... $25

First edition with dust jacket .... $50-$150

Golden Book of Fairy Tales, The

©1942

9 .... $40

First edition with dust jacket ....$50-$200

Golden Book of Flowers, The

©1943

16 .... $30

First edition with dust jacket ....$50-$150

Golden Egg Book, The

©1962

456 .... $7

Golden Goose, The

©1954

200 .... $12

487 .... $6

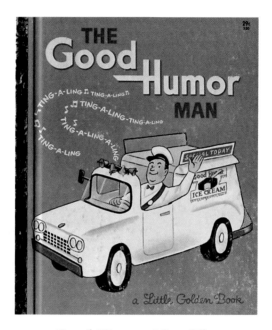

Good Humor Man, The

©1964

550 ....$75

Good Little, Bad Little Girl

©1965

562 .... $25

Good Morning, Good Night

©1948

61 .... $35

Good Night, Aunt Lilly

©1983

208-44......................$5

Good Night, Little Bear

©1961

447 ....$10

Good Old Days, The

©1988

204-58......................$5

Good-By Day, The

©1984

209-57......................$5

Good-bye, Tonsils
©1966

327 ....$7

Goofy—Movie Star
©1956

D52........................$18

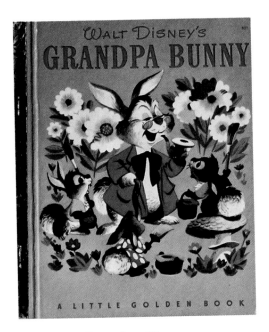

Grandpa Bunny

©1951

D21...............................$35

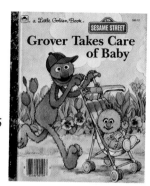

Grover Takes Care of Baby

©1987

109-57......................$5

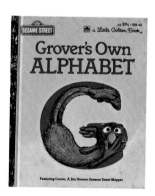

Grover's Own Alphabet

©1978

108-36......................$5

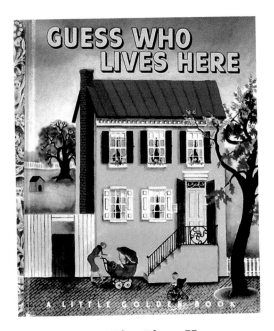

Guess Who Lives Here

©1949

60 ....$30

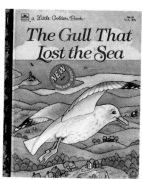

Gull That Lost the Sea, The

©1984

206-45.....................$5

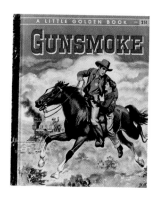

Gunsmoke

©1958

320 ....$20

Halloween
A B C

©1993

313-01 .... $3

Hansel and
Gretel

©1954

217 .... $8

491 .... $4

Hansel and Gretel

©1943

17.. $30
First edition with dust jacket............................$50-$150

Happy Birthday
©1952
123 .... $40

384 .... $15

Cut-out $3

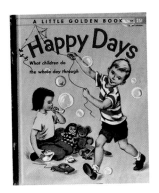

Happy Days
©1955
247 .... $10

Happy Family, The

©1947

35.. $40

First edition is unstated and lists to book #36 on back cover and dust jacket.

First edition with dust jacket...........................$50-$175

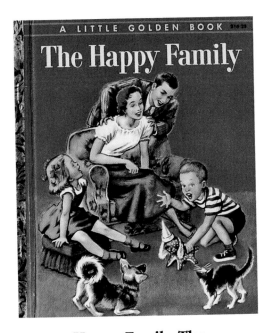

Happy Family, The

©1955

216 ....$16

Happy Golden A B C, The

©1972

344 .... $4

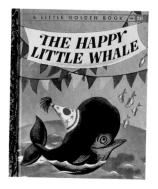

Happy Little Whale, The

©1960

393 .... $11

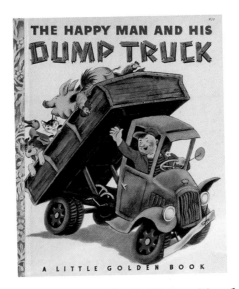

Happy Man and His Dump Truck, The

©1950

77 .... $20
520 .... $7
"B" edition with complete puzzle $150

Heidi

©1954

192 .... $8

258 .... $8

470 .... $6

Helicopters

©1959

357 .... $9

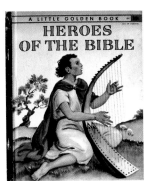

Heroes of the Bible

©1955

236 .... $11

Hey There—It's Yogi Bear

©1964

542 .... $18

Hiawatha
©1953
D31.......................$16

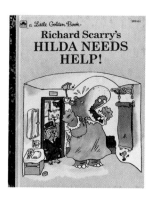

Hilda Needs Help!
©1993
208-64.....................$3

Hiram's Red Shirt

©1981

207-36......................$5

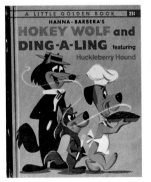

Hokey Wolf and Ding-A-Ling

©1961

444 ....$18

**Hop, Little
Kangaroo!**

©1965

558 .... $6

**Hopalong
Cassidy and the
Bar 20 Cowboy**

©1952

147 .... $25

House For a Mouse, A
©1990
304-63.....................$4

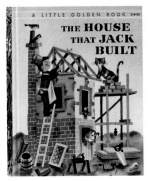

House That Jack Built, The
©1954
218 ....$11

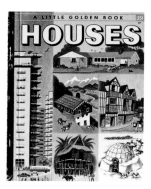

Houses
©1955
229 ....$10

How Big
©1949
83 ....$20

Second cover with dog
on cover $6

How Does Your Garden Grow?

©1985

308-55......................$5

How Things Grow

©1986

308-57......................$5

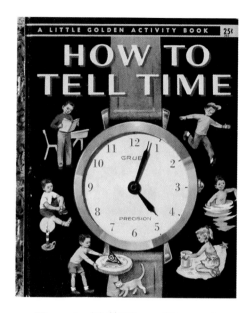

How to Tell Time (Gruen)

©1957

285.. $20
Non-Gruen edition with metal hands...................... $15

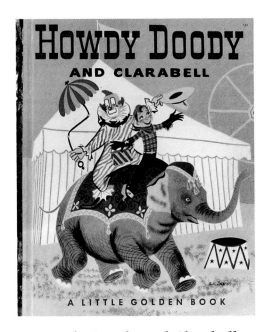

Howdy Doody and Clarabell

©1951

121 ....$25

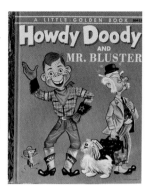

**Howdy Doody
and Mr. Bluster**
©1955
204 ....$25

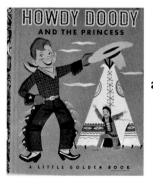

**Howdy Doody
and the Princess**
©1952
135 ....$25

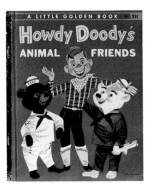

**Howdy Doody's
Animal Friends**
©1956
252 .... $25

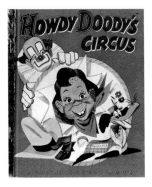

**Howdy Doody's
Circus**
©1950
99 .... $25

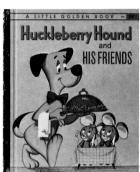

Huckleberry Hound and His Friends

©1960

406 ....$18

Huckleberry Hound—Safety Signs

©1961

458 ....$18

**Hurry-Up
Halloween
Costume, The**
©1997
98831 .... $2

**Hush, Hush, It's
Sleepytime**
©1968
577 .... $6

I Can Fly

©1950

92 .... $25

**I Can't Wait
Until Christmas**
©1989
456-10......................$5

**I Don't Want to
Go**
©1989
208-59......................$5

I Like to Live In the City
©1970
593 .... $7

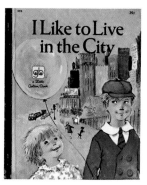

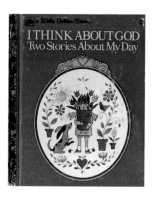

I Think About God—Two Stories About My Day
©1974
111 .... $6

If I Had A Dog

©1984

205-40.....................$5

Inspector Gadget In Africa

©1984

107-49......................$5

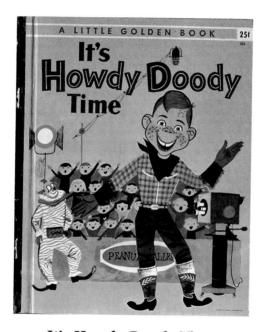

It's Howdy Doody Time

©1955

223 ....$25

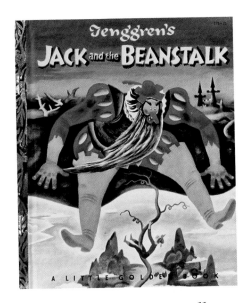

Jack and the Beanstalk

©1953

179 ....$15
281 ....$8
420 ....$6

Jack's Adventure

©1958

308 .... $10

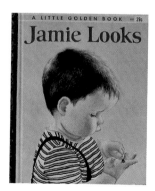

Jamie Looks

©1963

522 .... $18

Jenny's New Brother
©1970

596 .... $17

Jenny's Surprise Summer
©1981

204-39 .... $25

Jerry At School (Puzzle Edition)

©1950

94 .... $125

"B" non-puzzle
    edition $15

Jetsons, The

©1962

500 .... $25

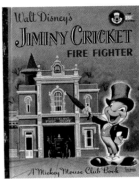

Jiminy Cricket— Fire Fighter
©1956
D50.........................$18

Jingle Bells
©1964
553 ....$7

Johnny Appleseed

©1949

D11.........................$18

Johnny's Machines

©1949

71 ....$16

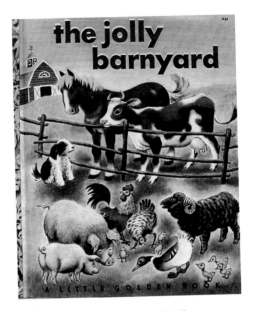

Jolly Barnyard, The

©1950

67 .... $16

"B" edition with complete puzzle $150

Jungle Book, The

©1967

D120........................$8

Just For Fun

©1960

264 ....$6

Just Watch Me!

©1975

104 .... $6

Katie the Kitten

©1949

75 .... $15

"E" edition with
complete
puzzle $125

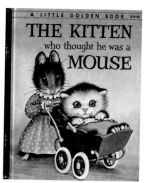

Kitten Who Thought He Was A Mouse, The

©1954

210 .... $18

Kitty's New Doll

©1984

210-63 .... $5

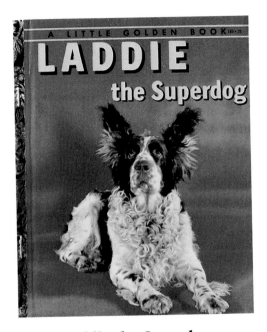

Laddie the Superdog

©1954

185 ....$12

Lady

©1954

D42...$16
D103...$7

**Lady Lovely
Locks—Silkypup
Saves the Day**

©1987

107-57 .... $5

**Land of the
Lost—The
Surprise Guests**

©1975

136 .... $10

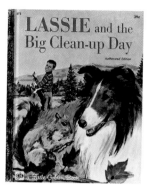

Lassie and the Big Clean-up Day

©1971

572 .... $6

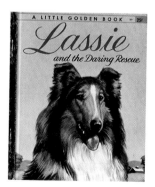

Lassie and the Daring Rescue

©1956

277 .... $16

Lassie Shows the Way

©1956

415 .... $7

518 .... $6

Leave It to Beaver

©1959

347 .... $25

Let's Fly A Kite, Charlie Brown!

©1987

111-62...................$5

Let's Go Shopping

©1948

33 ....$17

Let's Go Shopping!
©1988
208-58 .... $5

Let's Go to the Airport
©1997
98833 .... $5

Let's Go, Trucks!
©1973
185 .... $6

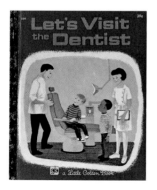

Let's Visit the Dentist
©1970
599 .... $6

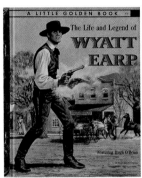

Life and Legend of Wyatt Earp, The

©1958

315 .... $18

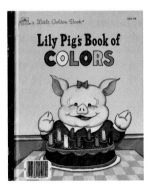

Lily Pig's Book of Colors

©1987

205-58 .... $5

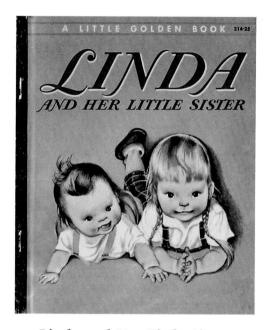

Linda and Her Little Sister

©1954

214 .... $75

Lion's Paw, The
©1959
367 .... $15

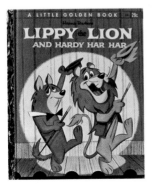

Lippy the Lion and Hardy Har Har
©1963
508 .... $18

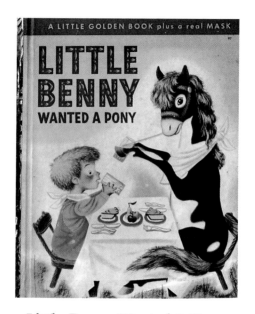

Little Benny Wanted A Pony

©1950

97 ....$60
Missing mask..........................$15

Little Black Sambo

©1948

57 ....$175
28-page edition $100
24-page edition $75

Little Book, The

©1969

583 .... $10

Little Boy and the Giant, The

©1973

536 .... $6

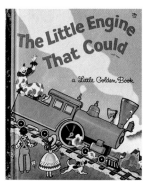

Little Engine That Could, The

©1954

548 .... $10

Little Eskimo, The

©1952

155 .... $16

Little Fat Policeman, The

©1950

91 ....$12

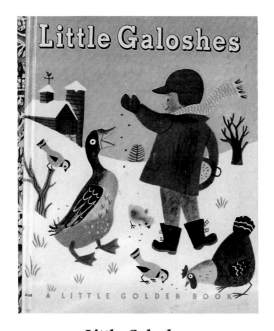

Little Galoshes

©1949

68 ....$25

Little Golden A B C, The

©1951

101 .... $125

Missing puzzle
.... $10

"B" non-puzzle
edition $8

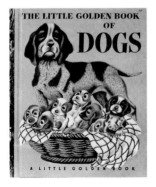

Little Golden Book of Dogs, The

©1952

131 .... $8

260 .... $8

Little Golden Holiday Book, The
©1951
109 ....$25

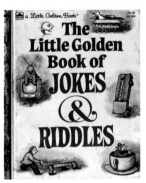

**Little Golden
Book of Jokes &
Riddles**

©1983

211-45...................... $5

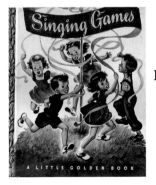

**Little Golden
Book of Singing
Games, The**

©1947

40 .... $15

Little Golden Funny Book, The

©1950

74 ....$14

Little Golden Mother Goose, The

©1957

283 ....$7

390 ....$6

472 ....$6

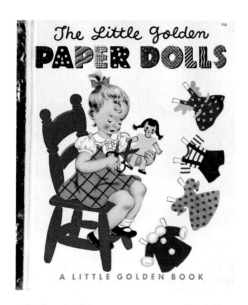

Little Golden Paper Dolls, The

©1951

113 ....$125
280 ....$125
Without clothes and dolls.........$5

Little Gray Donkey

©1954

206 ....$12

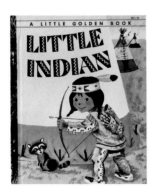

Little Indian

©1954

202 ....$15

Little Lost Kitten

©1979

302-56......................$3

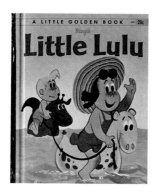

Little Lulu

©1962

476 ....$15

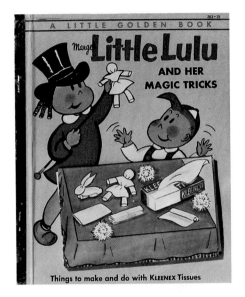

Little Lulu and Her Magic Tricks

©1954

203 ....$60
Without Kleenex® $25
Without table and Kleenex® ..$10

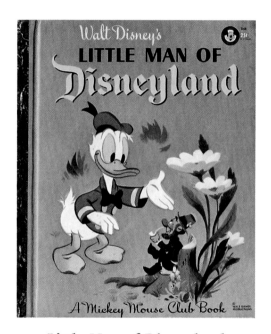

Little Man of Disneyland

©1955

D46...$16

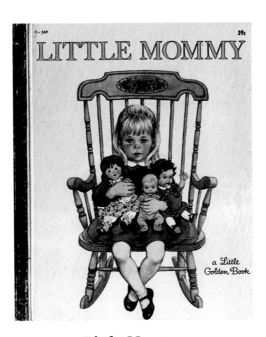

Little Mommy
©1967

569 ....$75

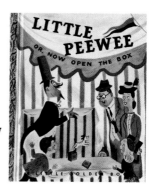

Little Pee Wee Or, Now Open the Box

©1948

52 .... $17

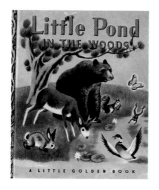

Little Pond In the Woods

©1948

43 .... $30

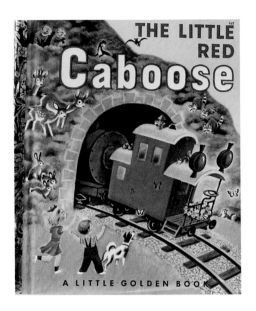

Little Red Caboose, The

©1953

162 ....$12
319 ....$10

Little Red Hen, The

©1942

6 .... $40

296 .... $7

First edition with dust
  jacket .... $50-$200

Little Red Hen, The

©1954

209 .... $8

519 .... $7

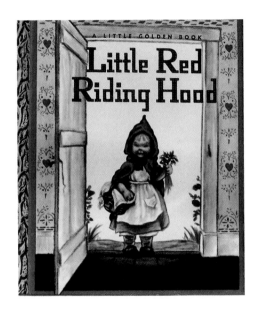

Little Red Riding Hood

©1948

42 .... $40
"G" edition with complete puzzle $150

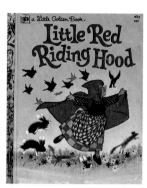

Little Red Riding Hood

©1972

232 .... $5

Little Red Riding Hood

©1985

307-59 .... $4

Little Red Riding Hood

©1992

300-65 .... $3

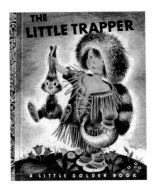

Little Trapper, The

©1950

79 .... $18

**Littlest
Christmas Elf,
The**
©1987
459-00.....................$5

Littlest Raccoon
©1961
457 ....$7

Lively Little Rabbit, The

©1943

15.. $35
551... $6
First edition with dust jacket............................ $50-$150

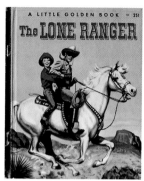

Lone Ranger, The

©1956

263 .... $22

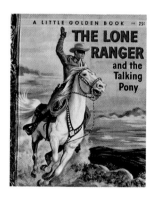

**Lone Ranger
and the Talking
Pony, The**

©1958

310 .... $20

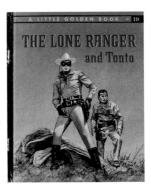

Lone Ranger and Tonto, The

©1957

297 .... $20

Loopy De Loop Goes West

©1960

417 .... $18

**Lord Is My
Shepherd, The—
The Twenty-
Third Psalm**

©1986

311-60......................$5

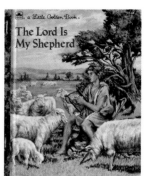

**Lost In the
Funhouse**

©1990

111-68......................$4

Love Bug, The—Herbie's Special Friend

©1974

D130..$11

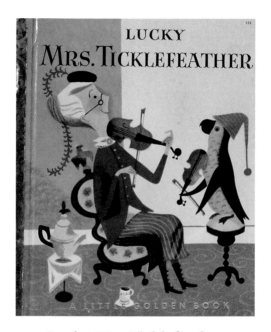

Lucky Mrs. Ticklefeather

©1951

122 ....$30

Lucky Puppy, The

©1960

D89..........................$13

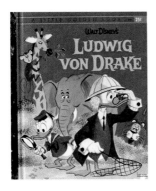

Ludwig Von Drake

©1961

D98..........................$15

Mad Hatter's Tea Party
©1952

D23.........................$16

Madeline
©1954

186 ....$18

Magic Compass, The

©1953

146 ....$20

Magic Friend-Maker, The

©1975

137 .... $15

Magic Next Door, The

©1971

106 .... $6

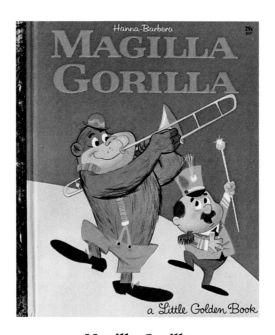

Magilla Gorilla

©1964

547 ....$18

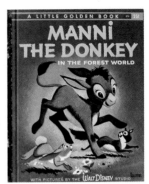

Manni the Donkey

©1959

D75.........................$13

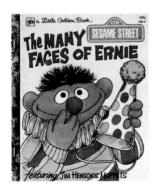

Many Faces of Ernie, The

©1979

109-4........................$5

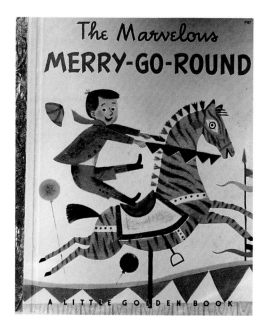

Marvelous Merry-Go-Round, The

©1949

87 ....$15

Mary Poppins

©1964

D113........................$12

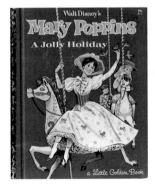

Mary Poppins—
A Jolly Holiday

©1964

D112........................$12

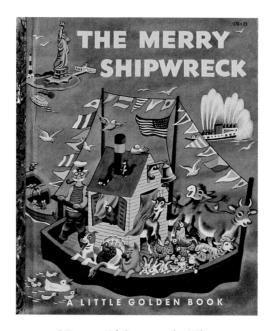

Merry Shipwreck, The

©1953

170 ....$15

Mickey Mouse and His Space Ship

©1952

D29...................$16

D108...................$10

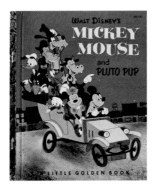

Mickey Mouse and Pluto Pup

©1953

D32...................$15

D76...................$8

**Mickey Mouse
and the Great
Lot Plot**

©1974

D129...........................$6

**Mickey Mouse
and the Missing
Mouseketeers**

©1956

D57.........................$12

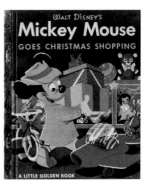

**Mickey Mouse
Goes Christmas
Shopping**

©1953

D33.........................$15

**Mickey Mouse
Heads For the
Sky**

©1987

100-60.......................$4

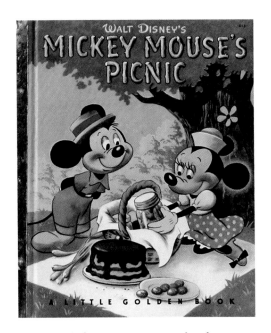

Mickey Mouse's Picnic

©1950

D15...$16

Mickey's Christmas Carol

©1983

459-42.....................$5

Minnie's Slumber Party

©1990

100-65.....................$3

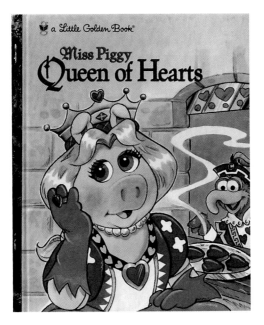

Miss Piggy—Queen of Hearts
©1997

98854 .... $2

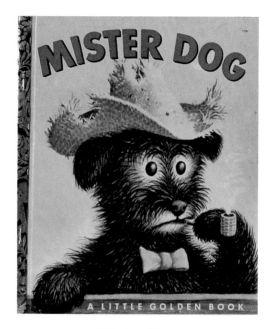

Mister Dog

©1952

128 ....$25

Monster At the End of This Book, The

©1971

316 ....$5

More Mother Goose Rhymes

©1958

317 ....$6

Mother Goose

©1942

4 ....$40

240 ....$12

First edition with dust
   jacket ....$50-$200

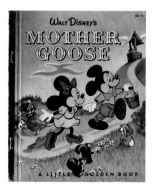

Mother Goose

©1952

D36.........................$35

D51..........................$8

D79.........................$8

Mother Goose In the City

©1974

336 ....$4

Mr. Bear's Birthday
©1981
204-26.....................$5

Mr. Bell's Fixit Shop
©1981
210-34.....................$5

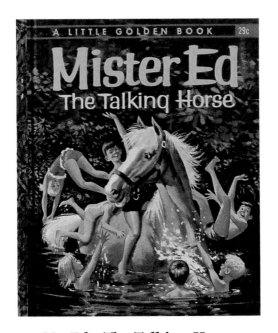

Mr. Ed—The Talking Horse

©1962

483 ....$20

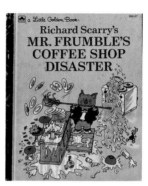

Mr. Frumble's Coffee Shop Disaster

©1993

208-67 .... $3

Mr. Noah and His Family

©1948

49 .... $18

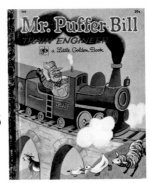

Mr. Puffer Bill Train Engineer

©1965

563 .... $6

Mr. Rogers' Neighborhood— Henrietta Meets Someone New

©1974

133 .... $6

Mr. Wigg's Birthday Party

©1952

140 .... $18

Musicians of Bremen, The

©1954

189 .... $8

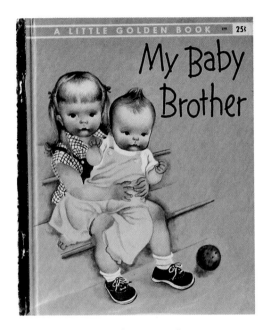

My Baby Brother
©1956

279 ....$25

My Baby Sister
©1958
340 .... $18

My Book of Poems
©1985
211-58 .... $4

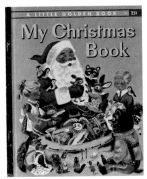

My Christmas Book

©1957

298 .... $17

My Christmas Treasury

©1976

144 .... $6

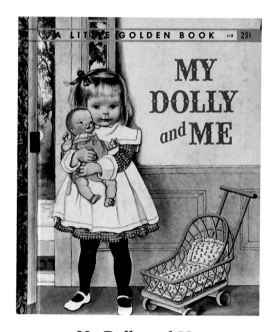

My Dolly and Me

©1960

418..$40

My First Book
(Second Cover)

©1942

10 .... $30

With dust
jacket .... $60-$150

My First Book
(Third Cover)

©1942

10 .... $20

First edition with dust
jacket .... $150-$250

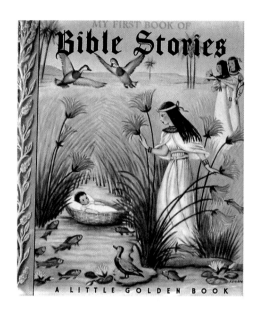

My First Book of Bible Stories

©1943

19... $40
First edition with dust jacket............................$60-$175

My Home
©1971
115 ....$6

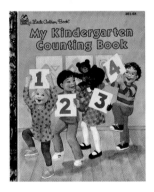

My Kindergarten Counting Book
©1995
301-68......................$3

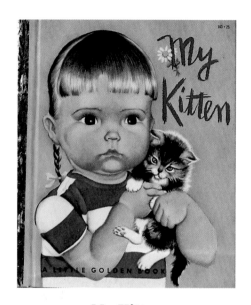

My Kitten

©1954

163 ....$18
300 ....$12
528 ....$10

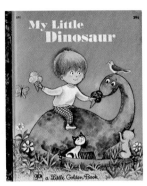

**My Little
Dinosaur**

©1971

571 .... $6

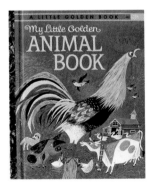

**My Little
Golden Animal
Book**

©1962

465 .... $7

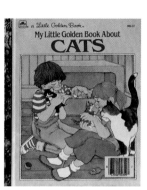

**My Little
Golden Book
About Cats**
©1988
309-57 .... $5

**My Little
Golden Book
About God**
©1956
268 .... $8

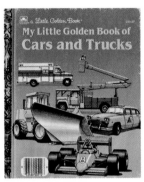

**My Little
Golden Book of
Cars and Trucks**

©1990

210-57......................$5

**My Little
Golden Book of
Fairy Tales**

©1990

211-62......................$3

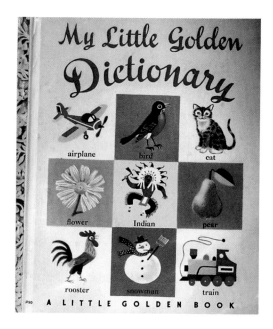

My Little Golden Dictionary

©1949

90 ....$15

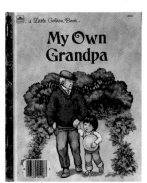

My Own Grandpa

©1987

208-56......................$5

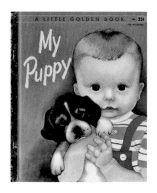

My Puppy

©1955

233 ....$15

469 ....$10

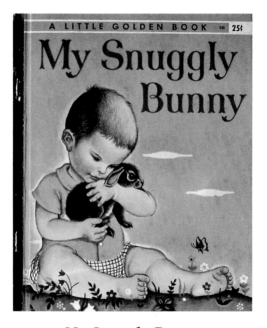

My Snuggly Bunny
©1956

250 ....$25

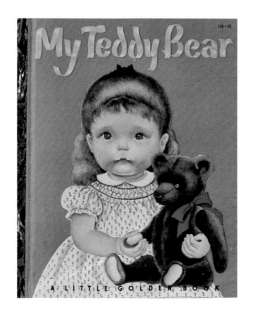

My Teddy Bear

©1953

168 ....$25
448 ....$20

My Word Book
©1963
525 ....$6

Neatos and the Litterbugs, The
©1973
515 ....$6

Never Pat A Bear—A Book About Signs

©1971

105 .... $6

New Baby, The

©1948

41 .... $40

291 .... $15

541 .... $8

Second cover "G" edition with boy looking into bassinet $15

New Baby, The
©1975
291 .... $14

New Baby, The
©1992
306-68 .... $3

New Brother, New Sister

©1966

564 ....$16

New House In the Forest, The

©1946

24.. $40

First edition is unstated and lists to book #27 on back cover and dust jacket.

First edition with dust jacket............................$50-$175

**New Kittens,
The**
©1957
302 .... $9

New Pony, The
©1961
410 .... $10

New Puppy, The
©1959

370 ....$7

Night Before Christmas, The

©1946

20 .... $25
Even though the first edition of this book has a blue
spine, it was never published with a dust jacket.
Second cover with Santa on roof $15
Third cover with Santa in fireplace and gilded $18
Third cover, "G" edition with Santa in fireplace $15

Night Before Christmas, The
©1955

241 ....$25

Noah's Ark
©1952
D28.........................$16

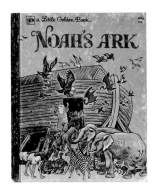

Noah's Ark
©1969
109 ....$6

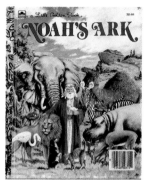

Noah's Ark
©1985
311-64.....................$5

Noel
©1991
456-16.....................$3

Noises and Mr. Flibberty-Jib

©1947

29 ....$40

Numbers

©1955

243 ....$6

337 ....$3

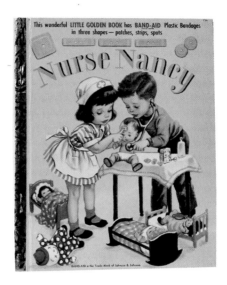

Nurse Nancy

©1952

154 ....$125
346 ....$125
473 ....$125
Without Band-Aids $40

Nursery Songs
©1942

7 .... $40

First edition with dust jacket .... $50-$200

Nursery Songs
©1959

348 .... $6

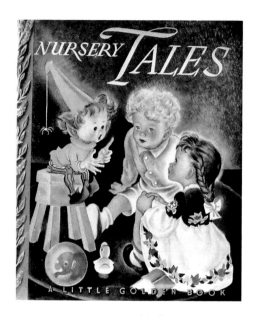

Nursery Tales

©1943

14... $25
First edition with dust jacket............................$50-$150

Nutcracker, The

©1991

460-15......................$4

Old Mother Goose and Other Nursery Rhymes

©1988

300-54......................$4

**Once Upon A
Wintertime**

©1950

D12..........................$20

**One of the
Family**

©1983

208-42......................$5

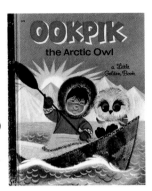

Ookpik, the Arctic Owl

©1968

579 .... $20

Open Up My Suitcase

©1954

207 .... $20

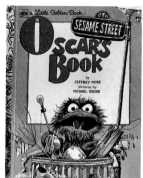

Oscar's Book
©1975
120 .... $5

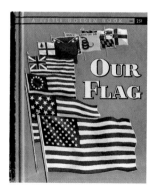

Our Flag
©1960
388 .... $6

Our World
©1955
242 ....$8

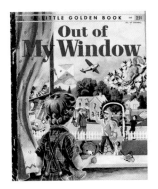

Out of My Window
©1955
245 ....$15

Pal and Peter
©1956
265 ....$10

Pantaloon
©1951
114 ....$25

This book can be found
with and without the
die-cut window.

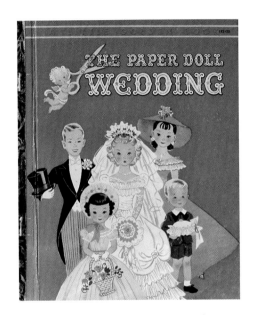

Paper Doll Wedding, The

©1954

193 ....$125
Without clothes and dolls $5

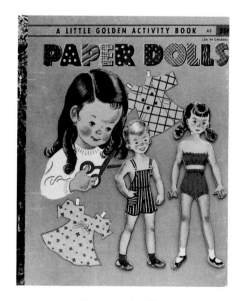

Paper Dolls

©1951

A3 ....$100
A47 ....$100
Without clothes and dolls........$5

**Party In
Shariland**

©1958

360 .... $17

Party Pig, The

©1954

191 .... $25

Paul Revere

©1957

D64..........................$12

Pebbles Flintstone

©1963

531 ....$20

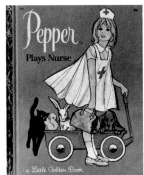

Pepper Plays Nurse
©1964
555 .... $18

Pete's Dragon
©1977
D137 .... $7

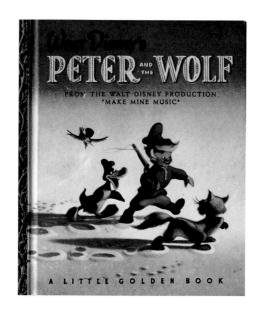

Peter and the Wolf

©1947

D5...$18
D56...$9

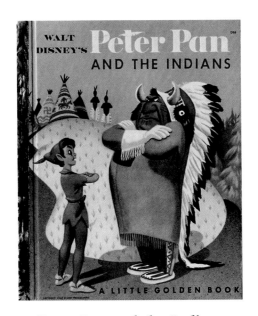

Peter Pan and the Indians

©1952

D26..$16
D74..$9

Peter Pan and the Pirates

©1952

D25......................$16

D73.........................$9

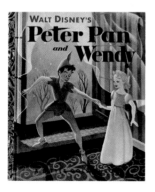

Peter Pan and Wendy

©1952

D24......................$16

D72.........................$9

D110.......................$7

Peter Potamus

©1964

556 ....$18

Peter Rabbit
©1958
313 .... $7
505 .... $7

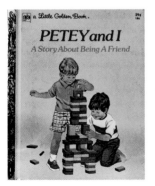

Petey and I—A Story About Being A Friend
©1973
186 .... $6

Pets For Peter (Puzzle Edition)

©1950

82 ....$100
Non-puzzle edition $14

Pick Up Sticks
©1962
461 ....$10

Pierre Bear
©1954
212 ....$30

Pierrot's A B C Garden
©1992
312-04.....................$4

Pink Panther In the Haunted House, The
©1975
140 ....$6

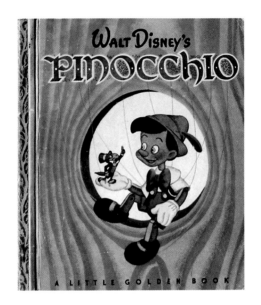

Pinocchio

©1948

D8..$18
D100..$8

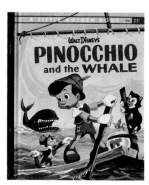

**Pinocchio and
the Whale**
©1961
D101......................$20

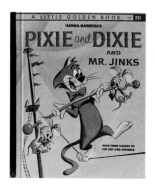

**Pixie and Dixie
and Mr. Jinks**
©1961
454 ....$35

Without cut-outs ... $10

Play Street
©1962
484 ....$17

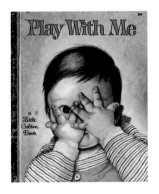

Play With Me
©1967
567 ....$15

Please and Thank You

©1997

98812 .... $3

Pluto and the Adventure of the Golden Scepter

©1972

D124 .... $6

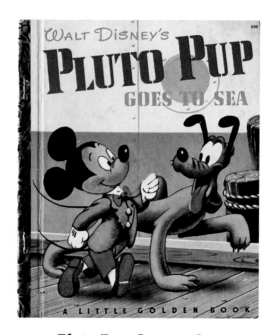

Pluto Pup Goes to Sea

©1952

D30...$16

Pocketful of Nonsense

©1992

312-05......................$4

Poky Little Puppy, The

©1942

8 ....$40

271 ....$7

506 ....$5

First edition with dust
jacket ....$50-$200

**Poky Little
Puppy Follows
His Nose Home,
The**

©1975

130 .... $6

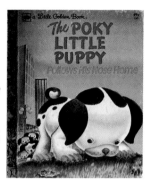

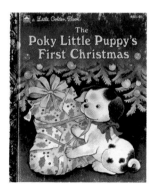

**Poky Little
Puppy's First
Christmas, The**

©1993

461-01 .... $4

**Poky Little
Puppy's
Naughty Day,
The**
©1985
303-57 .... $4

Polly's Pet
©1984
302-55 .... $4

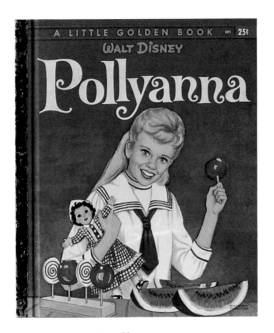

Pollyanna

©1960

D91...$20

**Porky Pig and
Bugs Bunny—
Just Like Magic!**

©1976

146 .... $6

**Prayers For
Children**

©1942

5 .... $40

First edition with dust
jacket ....$50-$200

Prayers For Children

©1952

205 .... $10

Puff the Blue Kitten

©1961

443 .... $18

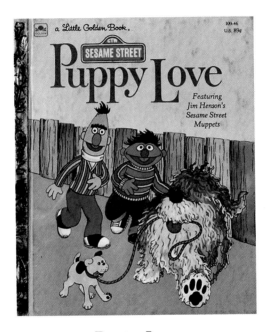

Puppy Love

©1983

109-46...$5

Puss In Boots

©1952

137 ....$11
359 ....$6

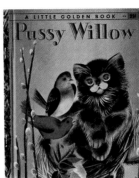

Pussy Willow

©1951

314 .... $10

Pussycat Tiger, The

©1972

362 .... $6

Quick Draw McGraw

©1960

398 ....$18

Rabbit and His Friends

©1953

169 .... $12

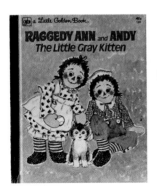

Raggedy Ann and Andy—The Little Gray Kitten

©1975

139 .... $6

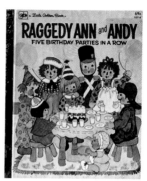

**Raggedy Ann
and Andy—Five
Birthday Parties
In a Row**

©1979

107-4........................$5

**Raggedy Ann
and Fido**

©1969

585 ....$6

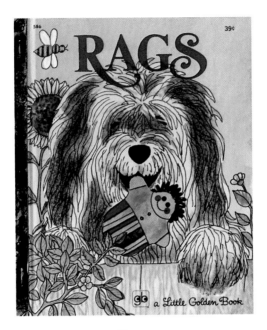

Rags

©1970

586 ....$7

Rainbow Brite and the Brook Meadow Deer

©1984

107-48......................$5

Rainy Day Play Book

©1981

206-35......................$5

Rainy Day Play Book

©1951

133 ....$18

Rapunzel
©1991
207-57......................$4

Ready, Set, Grow!
©1985
308-68......................$4

Red Little Golden Book of Fairy Tales, The

©1958

306 ....$13

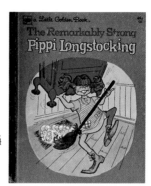

Remarkably Strong Pippi Longstocking, The

©1974

123 .... $14

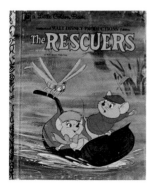

Rescuers, The

©1977

D136 .... $7

Return to Oz— Dorothy Saves the Emerald City

©1985

103-55.....................$9

Return to Oz— Escape From the Witch's Castle

©1985

105-56.....................$9

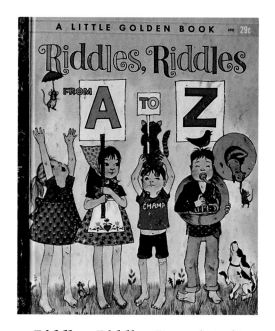

Riddles, Riddles From A to Z

©1962

490 ....$6

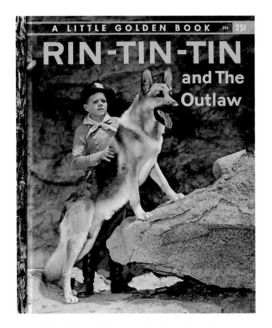

Rin-Tin-Tin and the Outlaw

©1957

304 ....$18

Road Runner, The—A Very Scary Lesson
©1974
122 .... $6

Road Runner, The—Mid-Mesa Marathon
©1985
110-57 .... $5

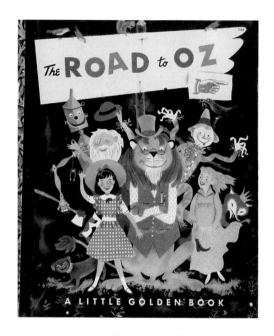

Road to Oz, The

©1951

144 ....$25

Robert and His New Friends

©1951

124 .... $15

Robin Hood

©1973

D126 .... $8

Robin Hood and the Daring Mouse

©1974

D128......................$10

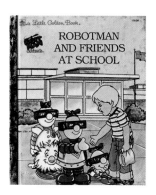

Robotman and Friends At School

©1985

110-58......................$5

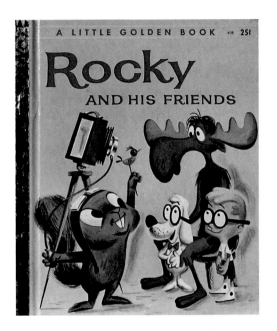

Rocky and His Friends

©1960

408 ....$20

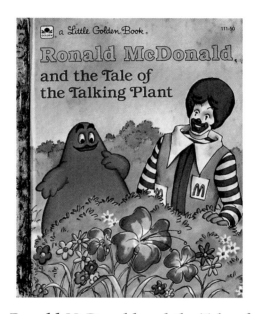

Ronald McDonald and the Tale of the Talking Plant

©1984

111-50.......................................$15

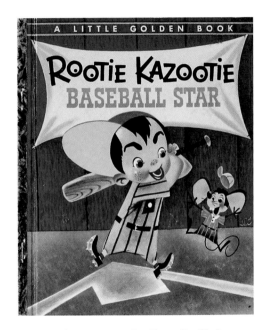

Rootie Kazootie Baseball Star

©1954

190 ....$30

Rootie Kazootie Detective

©1953

150 ....$25

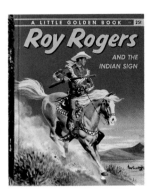

Roy Rogers and the Indian Sign

©1956

259 .... $22

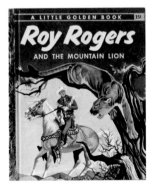

Roy Rogers and the Mountain Lion

©1955

231 .... $22

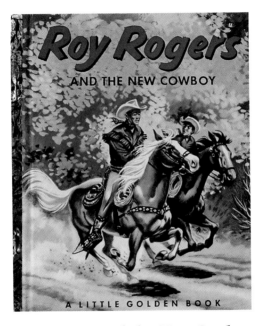

Roy Rogers and the New Cowboy

©1953

177 ....$22

Ruff and Reddy

©1959

378 .... $10

477 .... $10

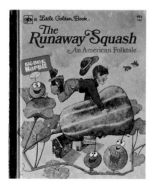

Runaway Squash, The

©1976

143 .... $6

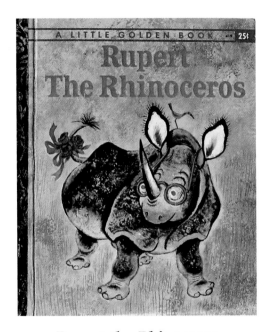

Rupert the Rhinoceros

©1960

419 ....$10

Rusty Goes to School

©1962

479 .... $15

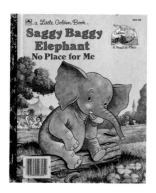

Saggy Baggy Elephant—No Place For Me

©1989

305-59 .... $4

Saggy Baggy Elephant, The

©1947

36 .... $25
385 .... $6

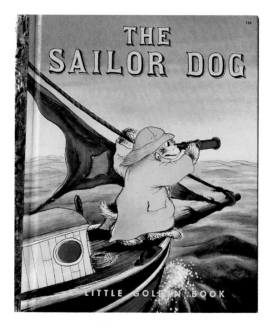

Sailor Dog, The

©1953

156 ....$25

Sam the Firehouse Cat

©1968

580 .... $7

Santa's Surprise Book

©1966

121 .... $6

Santa's Toy Shop

©1950

D16............................$16

Savage Sam

©1963

D104.......................$10

Scamp

©1957

D63.......................$12

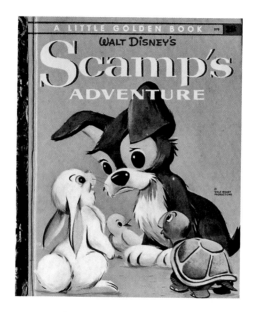

Scamp's Adventure

©1958

D70...$12
D88...$10

Scarebunny, The

©1985

209-59.....................$5

Scooby-Doo and the Pirate Treasure

©1974

126 ....$12

Scuffy the Tugboat

©1946

30.. $25
244.. $6
363.. $6
First edition is unstated and lists to book #34 on back
cover and #36 on dust jacket.
First edition with dust jacket............................$50-$150

Search for Christopher Robin, The

©1997

98841 .... $2

Sesame Street— The Together Book

©1971

315 .... $4

Seven Dwarfs Find A House

©1952

D35...........................$15

D67...........................$9

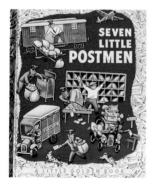

Seven Little Postmen

©1952

134 ....$18

504 ....$6

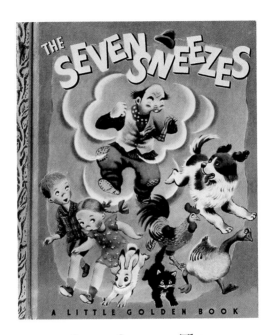

Seven Sneezes, The

©1948

51 ....$25

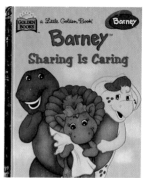

Sharing Is Caring

©1996

98790 .... $3

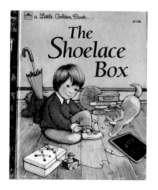

Shoelace Box, The

©1984

211-56 .... $5

Shy Little Kitten, The

©1946

23	$25
248	$7
494	$7

First edition is unstated and lists to book #27 on back cover and dust jacket.

First edition with dust jacket .... $50-$150

Silly Sisters, The
©1989
204-59......................$5

Sleeping Beauty and the Good Fairies
©1958
D71........................$12

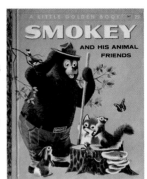

Smokey and His Animal Friends
©1960

387 .... $16

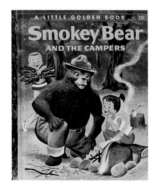

Smokey Bear and the Campers
©1961

423 .... $10

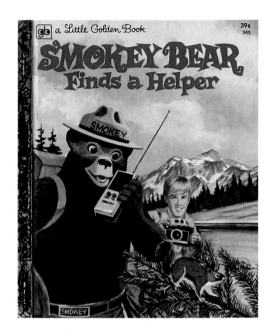

Smokey Bear Finds A Helper

©1972

345 ....$8

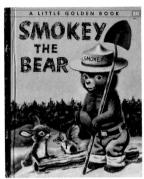

Smokey the Bear
©1955

224 .... $20

481 .... $11

Snoring Monster, The
©1985

208-55 .... $4

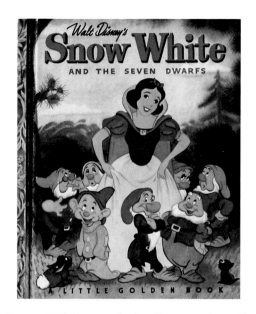

Snow White and the Seven Dwarfs

©1948

D4..$18
D66..$8

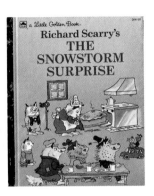

**Snowstorm
Surprise, The**

©1994

208-69.....................$3

So Big

©1968

574 ....$14

Soccer Coach
©1995
107-71......................$3

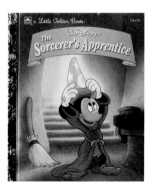

Sorcerer's Apprentice, The
©1994
100-79......................$3

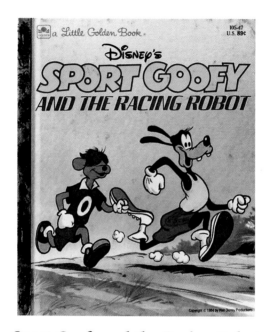

Sport Goofy and the Racing Robot

©1984

105-47...$8

Steve Canyon

©1959

356 ....$18

Store-Bought Doll, The

©1983

204-44......................$5

Stories of Jesus

©1974

114...........................$6

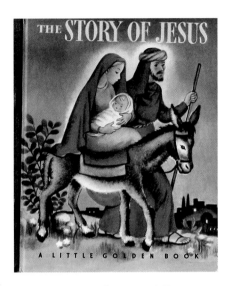

Story of Jesus, The

©1946

27.. $25

First edition is unstated and lists to book #34 on back cover and #36 on dust jacket.

First edition with dust jacket............................ $50-$150

Summer Vacation
©1986
206-56.....................$4

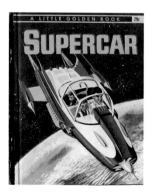

Supercar
©1962
492 ....$25

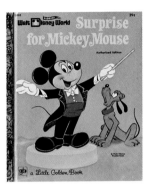

Surprise For Mickey Mouse

©1971

D105........................$5

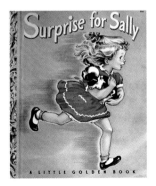

Surprise For Sally

©1950

84 ....$22

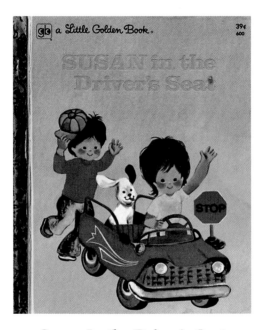

Susan In the Driver's Seat

©1973

600 ....$15

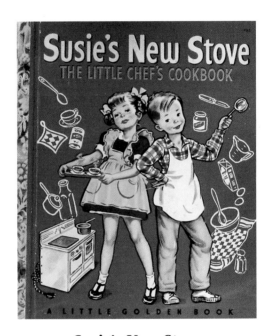

Susie's New Stove

©1950

85 ....$35

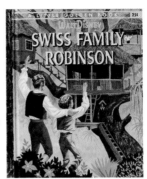

Swiss Family Robinson

©1961

D95.........................$14

Sword In the Stone, The

©1963

D106.......................$12

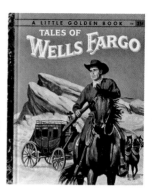

Tales of Wells Fargo
©1958
328 .... $20

Tarzan
©1964
549 .... $20

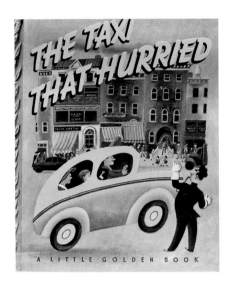

Taxi That Hurried, The

©1946

25.. $25
First edition is unstated and lists to book #27 on back
cover and dust jacket.
First edition with dust jacket............................$50-$150

Ten Items Or Less

©1985

203-54..$5

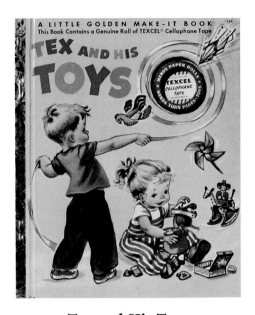

Tex and His Toys

©1952

129 ....$90
Without tape and activities.......$3

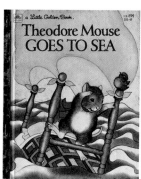

**Theodore Mouse
Goes to Sea**

©1983

201-45......................$5

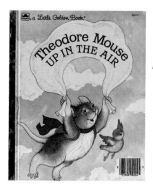

**Theodore Mouse
Up In the Air**

©1986

204-57......................$5

There Are Tyrannosaurs Trying On Pants In My Bedroom

©1991

209-64.................... $10

This Is My Family

©1992

312-02...................... $4

This Little Piggy and Other Counting Rhymes

©1942

12.. $50
First edition with dust jacket............................ $60-$250

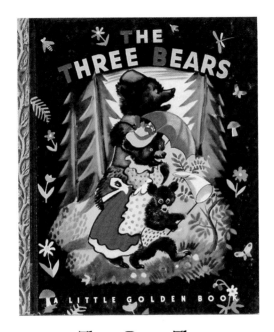

Three Bears, The

©1948

47 ....$150

Three Bears, The

©1948

47 .... $25

"B" edition

Three Bears, The

©1965

204 .... $6

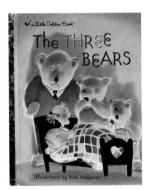

Three Bears, The

©2003

82576 .... $2.50

Three Bedtime Stories

©1958

309 .... $8

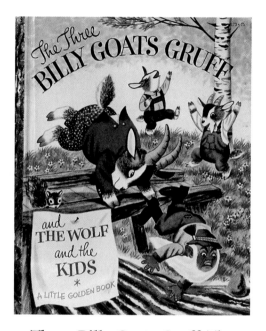

Three Billy Goats Gruff, The

©1953

173 .... $14

Three Little Kittens

©1942

1	$40
225	$7
288	$7
381	$6

First edition with dust jacket ....$50-$200

Three Little Pigs

©1948

D10	$18
D78	$11

Through the Picture Frame

©1944

D1...$45

First edition with dust jacket

....$50-$150

Thumbelina

©1953

153 ....$14
514 ....$6

**Tickety-Tock,
What Time Is It?**
©1990
308-51.....................$4

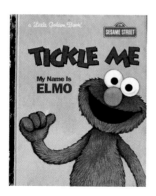

**Tickle Me—My
Name Is Elmo**
©1997
98837 ....$2

Tiger's Adventure

©1954

208 .... $11

351 .... $6

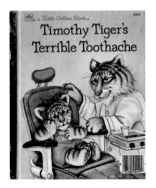

Timothy Tiger's Terrible Toothache

©1988

209-60 .... $5

Tin Woodman of Oz, The

©1952

159 ....$25

Tiny Dinosaurs
©1988
308-58......................$4

**Tiny, Tawny
Kitten, The**
©1969
590 ....$6

Toad Flies High
©1982
103-44......................$5

Toby Tyler
©1960
D87.......................$14

Tom and Jerry's Merry Christmas

©1954

197 .... $8

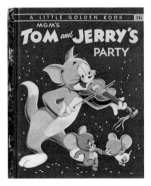

Tom and Jerry's Party

©1955

235 .... $7

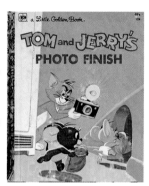

Tom and Jerry's Photo Finish

©1974

124 .... $10

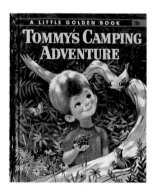

Tommy's Camping Adventure

©1962

471 .... $10

Tootle

©1945

21 .... $30

First edition with dust jacket .... $50-$175

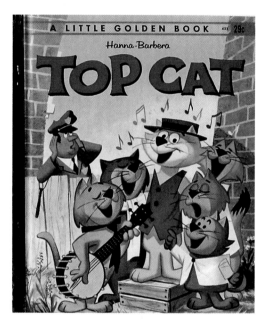

Top Cat

©1962

453 ....$20

**Topsy Turvy
Circus**

©1953

161 .... $15

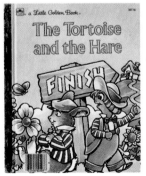

**Tortoise and the
Hare, The**

©1987

207-56 .... $5

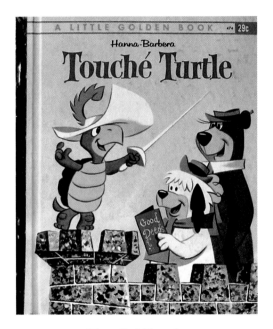

Touché Turtle

©1962

474 ....$20

Toy Soldiers, The—Babes in Toyland

©1961

D99..........................$12

Toys

©1945

22 ....$25

First edition with dust jacket ....$50-$150

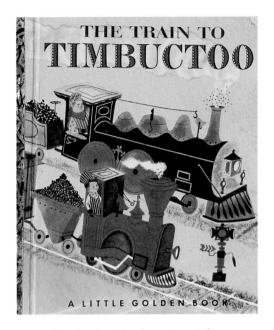

Train to Timbuctoo, The
©1951
118 ....$20

Travel
©1956
269 .... $7

Trick Or Treat
©1997
98838 .... $2

Trim the Christmas Tree

©1957

A15 ....$45
A50 ....$30
Without activities $3

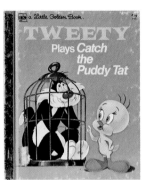

**Tweety Plays
Catch the Puddy
Tat**
©1975
141 ....$6

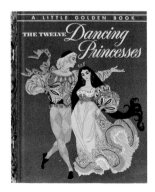

**Twelve Dancing
Princesses, The**
©1954
194 ....$25

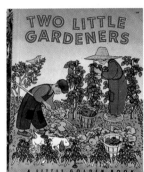

Two Little Gardeners

©1951

108 .... $15

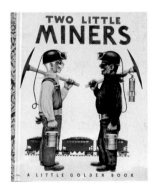

Two Little Miners

©1949

66 .... $30

Ugly Dachshund, The

©1966

D118......................$15

Ugly Duckling, The

©1952

D22........................$18

Ukelele and Her New Doll (Puzzle Edition)

©1951

102 .... $125
Without puzzle $25

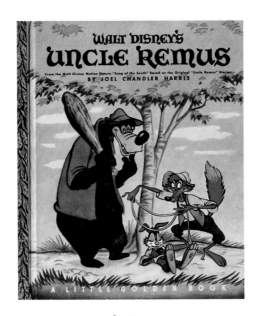

Uncle Remus

©1947

D6................................$25
D85..............................$10

Uncle Wiggily

©1953

148 .... $20

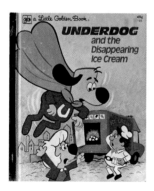

Underdog
and the
Disappearing
Ice Cream

©1975

135 .... $15

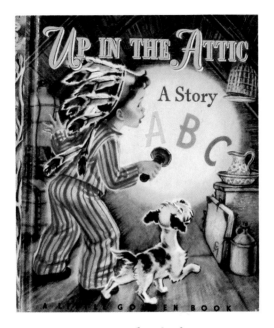

Up In the Attic

©1948

53 ....$18

**Velveteen
Rabbit, The**
©1992
307-68......................$4

**Visit to the
Children's Zoo,
A**
©1963
511 ....$7

Wacky Witch

©1973

416 .... $10

Wake Up, Groundhog!

©1997

98848 .... $2

Wally Gator

©1963

502 ....$18

Waltons and the Birthday Present, The

©1975

134 .... $6

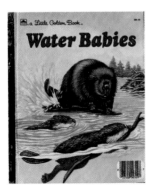

Water Babies

©1990

309-59 .... $4

We Help Mommy
©1959

352 ....$15

**We Like
Kindergarten**
©1965
552 ....$6

**We Like to Do
Things**
©1949
62 ....$14

Whales
©1978
171 .... $7

What Am I?
©1949
509 .... $6

What If?
©1951

130 ....$12

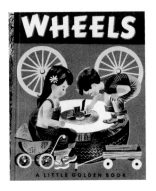

Wheels
©1952

141 ....$14

When I Grow Up

©1968

578 ....$6

When I Grow Up (Puzzle Edition)

©1950

96 ....$125

"B" non-puzzle
edition.................$15

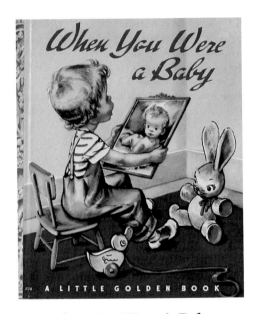

When You Were A Baby

©1949

70 ....$17

435 ....$6

**When You Were
A Baby**
©1982
209-39......................$3

**Where Did the
Baby Go?**
©1974
116 ....$11

Where Is the Bear?
©1967
568 .... $6

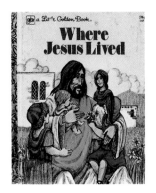

Where Jesus Lived
©1977
147 .... $6

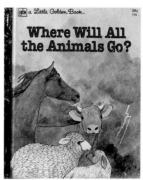

**Where Will All
the Animals Go?**

©1978

175 .... $6

**Whispering
Rabbit, The**

©1992

312-03...................... $3

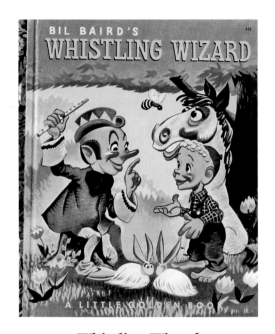

Whistling Wizard

©1953

132 ....$18

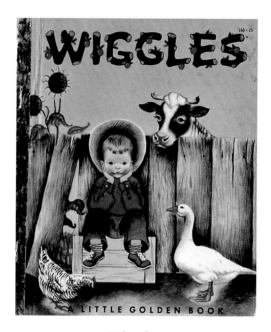

Wiggles

©1953

166 ....$30

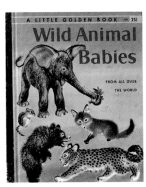

Wild Animal Babies

©1958

332 .... $6

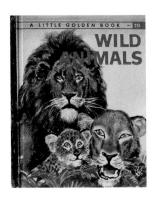

Wild Animals

©1961

394 .... $6

499 .... $5

Wild Kingdom
©1976
151 .... $6

Willie Found a Wallet
©1984
205-56 .... $5

Winky Dink

©1956

266 ....$20

Winnie the Pooh—Eeyore, Be Happy!
©1991
102-62......................$3

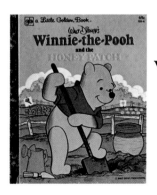

Winnie-the-Pooh and the Honey Patch
©1980
101-4........................$5

Winnie-the-Pooh and the Honey Tree
©1965
D116..........................$8

Winnie the Pooh and the Missing Bullhorn
©1990
101-55......................$5

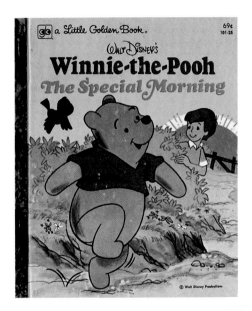

Winnie-the-Pooh and the Special Morning

©1980

101-25...$8

Winnie-the-Pooh
and Tigger
©1968

D121..........................$7

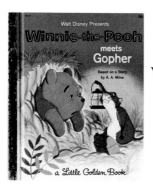

Winnie-the-Pooh
Meets Gopher
©1972

D117..........................$7

Wizard of Oz, The

©1975

119 .... $8

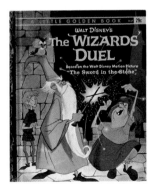

Wizards' Duel, The

©1963

D107 .... $15

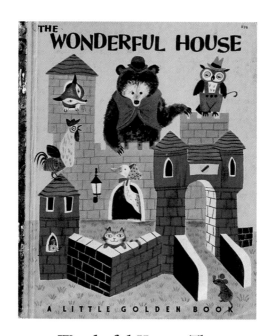

Wonderful House, The

©1950

76 ....$17

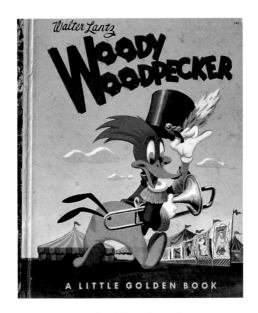

Woody Woodpecker

©1952

145 ....$11
330 ....$6

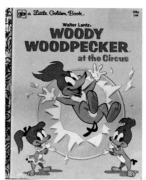

**Woody
Woodpecker At
the Circus**
©1976
149 .... $6

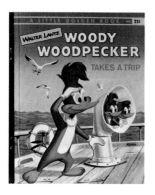

**Woody
Woodpecker
Takes a Trip**
©1961
445 .... $7

Woody Woodpecker—Drawing Fun For Beginners

©1959

372 ....$20

Words (Wheel Book)

©1955

A1	$30
A30	$25
Without wheel	$6

**Xavier's
Birthday
Surprise!**
©1987
107-64......................$5

**Yakky Doodle
and Chopper**
©1962
449 .... $20

Year In the City, A

©1948

48 ....$25

Yogi Bear
©1960
395 .... $18

Yogi Bear—A Christmas Visit
©1961
433 .... $18

More Little Golden Books

The following titles were not shown in the previous section.

Title	Book Number	Value
101 Dalmatians	105-65	$4
12 Days of Christmas, The	526	$8
A B C Around the House	200-5	$4
Adventure In Beggar's Canyon	98879	$2
Adventures of Goat	201-10	$3
Airplanes	180	$10
Aladdin—The Magic Carpet Ride	107-92	$3
Ali Baba	323	$12
All Aboard	152	$16
Anastasia	98805	$2
Animal Counting Book	584	$5
Animal Daddies and My Daddy	576	$5
Animal Gym, The	249	$14
Animal Orchestra	334	$8
Animal Paint Book	A4	$55
Animal Stamps	A7	$30
Animals ABC's	202-65	$2
Animals and Their Babies	A29	$25
Animals' Christmas Eve, The	154	$6
Annabelle's Wish	98843	$2

Title	Book Number	Value
Another Monster at the End of This Book	98769	$3
Arthur's Good Manners	305-58	$5
Baby Animals	274	$7
Baby Brown Bear's Big Bellyache	304-64	$5
Baby Fonzie Visits the Doctor	111-89	$3
Baby Jesus Stamps	A12	$150
Baby Sister	306-55	$5
Baby's First Christmas	368	$12
Bambi—Friends of the Forest	D132	$6
Barbie and the Scavenger Hunt	107-96	$4
Bear In the Boat, The	397	$5
Bears' New Baby, The	306-57	$5
Benji—Fastest Dog In the West	165	$5
Berts Hall of Great Inventions	109-3	$2
Best Christmas Eve!, The (Barney)	98815	$2
Best of All!, The—A Story About the Farm	170	$5
Best Thanksgiving Day, The (Pooh)	96009	$2
Betsy McCall	559	$75
Bible Heroes	82816	$2.50
Big Bird Meets Santa Claus	98814	$3
Big Bird Visits Navajo Country	108-68	$3
Big Bird's Baby Book	98865	$2
Big Bird's Day On the Farm	107-61	$5

Title	Book Number	Value
Big Bird's Red Book	157	$6
Big Bird's Ticklish Christmas	98839	$2
Big Splash, The (Barbie)	107-86	$4
Big, Terrible Trouble? (Power Puff Girls)	99500	$3
Biggest, Most Beautiful Christmas Tree, The	459-8	$3
Bird Stamps	A8	$40
Birds	184	$7
Black Caldron, The —Taran Finds A Friend	105-54	$5
Black Hole, The	501	$5
Blessing From Above, A	82866	$3
Bob the Builder	82714	$3
Bobby and His Airplanes	69	$18
Bobby, the Hopping Robot	98657	$3
Boo-o-s On First (Casper and Friends)	107-85	$3
Bouncy Baby Bunny Finds His Bed, The	129	$6
Boy and the Tiger, The	82719	$3
Bozo and the Hide 'n' Seek Elephant	598	$8
Broken Arrow	299	$17
Brother Bear	2176	$3
Buck Rogers and the Children of Hopetown	500	$5
Bugs Bunny and the Health Hog	110-60	$5

Title	Book Number	Value
Bugs Bunny at the Easter Party	183	$14
Bugs Bunny Calling!	111-70	$5
Bugs Bunny Marooned!	110-55	$5
Bugs Bunny Party Pest	111-69	$4
Bugs Bunny Pirate Island	110-52	$4
Bugs Bunny Stowaway	110-66	$4
Bugs Bunny's Carrot Machine	127	$6
Bugs Bunny, Pioneer	161	$6
Bugs Bunny—Too Many Carrots	145	$6
Bunnies' ABC	202-56	$3
Bunny Hop, The (Sesame Street)	98791	$2
Bunny's Magic Tricks	441	$14
Busiest Fire Fighters Ever!	208-66	$2
Buster Cat Goes Out	302-57	$5
Captain Kangaroo	261	$12
Captain Kangaroo and the Beaver	427	$8
Captain Kangaroo's Surprise Party	341	$12
Car and Truck Stamps	A20	$40
Cars and Trucks	366	$6
Cat In the Hat, The	82491	$3
Catch That Hat! (Barney)	98807	$2
Cave Kids	539	$25

Title	Book Number	Value
Chelli and the Great Sandbox Adventure	98818	$2
Christmas Donkey, The	460-9	$2
Christmas Tree That Grew, The	458-1	$4
Christopher and the Columbus	103	$12
Cinderella (Barbie)	96040	$3
Cinderella (Paper Dolls)	A36	$150
Cindy Bear	442	$18
Circus Is In Town, The	168	$5
Circus Time (Wheel Book)	A2	$25
Cleo	287	$14
Clown Coloring Book	A5	$75
Color Kittens, The	202-66	$3
Colors (Wheel Book)	A28	$35
Cookie Monster and the Cookie Tree	159	$6
Corky	486	$12
Cow and the Elephant, The	304-48	$5
Cow Went Over the Mountain, The	516	$6
Cowboy ABC	389	$12
Cowboy Stamps	A11	$45
Creature Teacher (Power Puff Girls)	96011	$3
Daddies—All About the Work They Do	201-69	$2
Dan Yaccarino's Mother Goose	82571	$3

Title	Book Number	Value
Daniel Boone	256	$12
Darby O'Gill	D81	$16
Day In the Jungle, A	18	$35
Day On the Farm, A	407	$6
Dennis the Menace and Ruff	386	$12
Doctor Dan At the Circus	399	$100
Doctor Dan, the Bandage Man	295	$125
Dog Stamps	A9	$45
Donald Duck and the Big Dog	102-55	$4
Donald Duck and the Mouseketeers	D55	$16
Donald Duck and the One Bear	D139	$6
Donald Duck and the Private Eye	D94	$16
Donald Duck—Lost and Found	D86	$15
Double Trouble: A Story About Twins	96001	$3
Dr. Ruth: Grandma on Wheels	98239	$3
Dragon In a Wagon, A	565	$5
Duck Tales—The Hunt For the Giant Pearl	102-58	$4
Duck Tales—The Secret City Under the Sea	102-57	$4
Eeyore, You're the Best!	98765	$2
Elmo's New Puppy	98897	$2
Elmo's Tricky Tongue Twister	98871	$2

Title	Book Number	Value
Eloise Wilkin's Mother Goose	589	$5
Emerald City of Oz	151	$27
Enchanted Christmas, The (Beauty and the Beast)	98828	$2
Ernie's Work of Art	109-5	$2
Farm Stamps	A19	$35
Farmyard Friends	272	$7
Feelings From A to Z	200-6	$5
Finding Nemo	2139	$3
Fireman & Fire Engine Stamps	A27	$45
First Steps	98896	$6
Fix It Please	32	$35
Flying Car, The	D96	$15
Forest Hotel	350	$5
Four Puppies	405	$6
Four Seasons, The	108-4	$2
Fox and the Hound—Hide & Seek (Unstated First)	105-26	$5
Fox Jumped Up One Winter's Night, A	300-53	$5
Fozzie's Fabulous Easter Parade	98849	$2
Fozzie's Funnies	111-87	$3
Fritzie Goes Home	103	$7
From Then to Now	201	$10

Title	Book Number	Value
From Trash to Treasure	108-70	$3
Frosty Day, A	99509	$3
Funny Bunny	304-59	$3
Garfield—The Cat Show	110-61	$4
Garfield and the Space Cat	107-65	$4
Gerald McBoing Boing	82721	$3
Gift of Christmas, The	98802	$2
Golden Sleepy Book	46	$25
Goliath II	D83	$15
Gordon's Jet Flight (Paper Model Jet)	A48	$150
Grand and Wonderful Day, The	101-64	$2
Grandma and Grandpa Smith	305-55	$5
Great Egg-Spectations—Goof Troop	107-87	$6
Great Riddle Contest, The (Pooh)	98915	$3
Grover's Guide to Good Manners	109-66	$3
Growing Up Grouchy (Sesame Street)	98794	$2
Hansel and Gretel (Paper Dolls)	A41	$150
Happy and Sad, Grouch and Glad (Sesame Street)	108-67	$3
Happy Birthday Babs! (Tiny Toon Adventures)	111-67	$4
Happy Farm Animals, The	200-54	$3
Happy Holiday, A (Barbie)	96004	$3

Title	Book Number	Value
Haunted Carnival, The (Scooby-Doo!)	99504	$3
Haunted Halloween	96006	$6
Haunted Tracks, The	99511	$5
Hercules	98800	$2
Hercules—A Race to the Rescue	98801	$2
Here Comes the Parade	143	$16
Hi! Ho! Three In a Row	188	$27
Ho-Ho-Ho, Baby Fozzie!	98817	$2
Holiday Helpers (Barbie)	96000	$2
Home For a Bunny	428	$8
Home On the Range	2214	$3
Horses	459	$6
How the Camel Got Its Hump	96019	$3
How the Leopard Got Its Spots	99501	$3
How the Turtle Got Its Shell	96007	$3
How the Zebra Got Its Stripes	98870	$3
Howdy Doody and His Magic Hat	184	$25
Howdy Doody and Santa Claus	237	$27
Howdy Doody In Funland	172	$24
Howdy Doody's Lucky Trip	171	$25
Huckleberry Hound Builds a House	376	$18
Huckleberry Hound and the Christmas Sleigh	403	$18

Title	Book Number	Value
Hunchback of Notre Dame, The	107-35	$2
Hungry Little Puppies	98882	$4
I Have a Secret	495	$8
I Love You, Daddy!	99508	$3
I Love You, Mommy!	99507	$3
I Think That It Is Wonderful	109-9	$3
I'm an Indian Today	425	$8
In the Spotlight (Barbie)	98863	$2
Indian Stamps	A13	$40
Indian, Indian	149	$16
Insect Stamps	A25	$35
J. Fred Muggs	234	$17
Jewel Thief, The (Barbie)	98864	$3
Just a Bad Day	98873	$2
Just a Little Different	98875	$2
Just Imagine—A Book of Fairyland Rhymes	211-61	$4
Just Like Dad	98876	$2
Just Say Please	96017	$2
Kermit, Save the Swamp!	111-84	$3
King Midas and the Golden Touch	98810	$2
King of the Beasties (Pooh)	98820	$2

Title	Book Number	Value
Kitten's Surprise, The	107	$12
Kitty On the Farm	200-57	$3
Laddie and the Little Rabbit	116	$12
Lady and the Tramp	105-55	$2
Large and Growly Bear, The	510	$8
Lassie and Her Day In the Sun	307	$9
Lassie and the Lost Explorer	343	$12
Let's Be Thankful	96022	$3
Let's Go to the Dairy Farm	98224	$6
Let's Go to the Fire Station	98802	$2
Let's Go to the Vet	98804	$3
Let's Play Ball	325	$12
Let's Save Money (Wheel Book)	A21	$18
Lion King, The	107-93	$3
Lion's Mixed-Up Friends	304-62	$5
Little Mouse's Book of Colors	211-71	$3
Little Boy With a Big Horn	100	$16
Little Brown Bear	304-60	$5
Little Cottontail	414	$6
Little Crow	113	$7
Little Golden Book of Hymns, The	34	$16
Little Golden Book of Poetry, The	38	$16

Title	Book Number	Value
Little Golden Book of Words, The	45	$18
Little Golden Picture Dictionary	369	$5
Little Golden Picture Dictionary	96035	$2
Little Mermaid, The	105-68	$4
Little Pee Wee, the Circus Dog Or, Now Open the Box	52	$25
Little Pussycat	302-51	$5
Little Red Riding Hood (Paper Dolls)	A34	$175
Little Yip-Yip and His Bark	73	$16
Machines	455	$6
Make Way For the Thruway	439	$12
Maverick	354	$18
Me Cookie!	109-69	$3
Meltdown On Hoth (Star Wars)	98202	$2
Mewtwo Strikes Back	98916	$3
Mickey and the Beanstalk	103-59	$4
Mickey Mouse—Those Were the Days	100-61	$4
Mickey Mouse and Goofy—The Big Bear Scare	D138	$6
Mickey Mouse and the Best Neighbor Contest	D134	$6
Mickey Mouse and the Mouseketeers— Ghost Town Adventure	D135	$6
Mickey Mouse Club Stamp Book	A10	$75

Title	Book Number	Value
Mickey Mouse Flies the Christmas Mail	D53	$16
Mickey Mouse—The Kitten Sitters	D133	$6
Mickey's Walt Disney World Adventure	98842	$5
Mike and Melissa (Paper Dolls)	A31	$125
Mike's Dirty, Yucky, Icky, Sticky Adventure	99810	$8
Missing Wedding Dress Featuring Barbie, The	107-63	$6
Mississippi Skip	96021	$3
Mommies—All About the Work They Do	98811	$2
Monsters' Picnic, The	109-59	$3
Moving Day (Formerly: The Good-by Day)	209-57	$5
Mrs. Brisby and the Magic Stone	110-38	$6
Mulan	98861	$2
Muppet Treasure Island	111-88	$3
My First Book of Planets	308-56	$5
My First Book of Sounds (Formerly: Bow Wow! Meow!)	205-54	$3
My First Counting Book	434	$5
My Little Golden Book About Dogs	309-71	$5
My Little Golden Book of Jokes	424	$6
My Little Golden Book of Manners	460	$6
My Little Golden Calendar	A39	$90
My Little Golden Word Book	305-53	$3

Title	Book Number	Value
Name For Kitty, A	55	$14
National Velvet	431	$14
Naughty Bunny, The	377	$27
New Baby, The (Second Cover)	41	$15
New Friends For the Saggy Baggy Elephant	131	$7
New Kid In School (McKids)	98886	$2
No Worries (The Lion King)	107-97	$3
Nursery Rhymes	59	$14
Nutcracker, The (Barbie)	99512	$3
Oh, Little Rabbit!	304-50	$5
Old MacDonald Had a Farm	400	$6
Old Mother Hubbard	591	$5
Old Yeller	D65	$15
Oscar's New Neighbor	109-67	$3
Our Puppy	292	$7
Owl and the Pussy Cat, The	300-41	$5
Pano the Train	117	$7
Pat-a-Cake	54	$14
Perri and Her Friends	D54	$16
Peter Cottontail and the Great Mitten Hunt	99505	$3
Peter Cottontail Is on His Way	99506	$3

Title	Book Number	Value
Peter Pan	104-60	$4
Pied Piper, The	300-57	$3
Pink Panther and Sons—Fun at the Picnic	111-60	$4
Pocahontas—The Voice of the Wind	104-72	$2
Pocahontas (Unstated First)	104-71	$2
Poky Little Puppy Comes to Sesame Street, The	98781	$2
Poky Little Puppy's Special Day	200-58	$3
Pony For Tony, A	220	$12
Pooh and the Dragon	98798	$2
Pound Puppies—Problem Puppies	111-61	$4
Pound Puppies In Pick of the Litter	110-59	$4
Prince and the Pauper, The	105-71	$4
Princess and the Pea, The	207-68	$3
Puppy On the Farm (Previously: Duffy On the Farm)	304-52	$4
Put On a Happy Face	107-84	$3
Quasimodo the Hero	98797	$2
Quasimodo's New Friend	107-36	$2
Quints—The Cleanup	107-72	$3
Rabbit Is Next, The	173	$5
Rabbit's Adventure, The	164	$6

Title	Book Number	Value
Raggedy Ann and Andy and the Rainy Day Circus	401	$5
Raggedy Ann and Andy Help Santa Claus	156	$6
Raggedy Ann and Santa Claus (Unstated First)	156	$6
Raggedy Ann and the Cookie Snatcher	262	$6
Rainbow Puppies (101 Dalmatians)	98858	$2
Reading, Writing & Spelling Stamps	A24	$40
Ready, Set, Go! A Counting Book	109-71	$3
Rescuers Down Under, The	105-70	$4
Right's Animal Farm	200-9	$5
Rin Tin Tin and Rusty	246	$18
Rin Tin Tin and the Lost Indian	276	$17
Romper Room Do Bees	273	$8
Romper Room Exercise Book, The	527	$8
Rootie Kazootie Joins the Circus	226	$25
Roy Rogers and Cowboy Toby	195	$22
Rudolph the Red-Nosed Reindeer	331	$12
Rudolph the Red-Nosed Reindeer Shines Again	460-31	$5
Rudolph the Red-Nosed Reindeer: Oh Nose!	96005	$3
Rumpelstiltskin (Formerly Red LGB of Fairy Tale)	300-56	$5

Title	Book Number	Value
Rumpelstiltskin and the Princess and the Pea	498	$8
School Play, The	98813	$3
Sesame Street Mother Goose Rhymes	108-69	$3
Shaggy Dog, The	D82	$15
Shall We Dance? A Book of Opposites	96002	$2
Shazam! A Circus Adventure	155	$6
Shy Little Kitten's Secret Place	302-58	$4
Sing With Me—My Name Is Ernie	98856	$3
Sky, The	270	$8
Sleeping Beauty	D61	$15
Sleeping Beauty (Barbie)	10602	$3
Sleeping Beauty (Paper Dolls)	A33	$175
Sleepytime A B C	202-57	$3
Sly Little Bear	411	$8
Snow Day!	98619	$3
Snow Puppies (101 Dalmatians)	98786	$2
Snow White and Rose Red	228	$14
Special Sleepover, The (Barbie)	98808	$2
Stop and Go (Wheel Book)	A17	$40
Sweetest Christmas, The (Pooh)	98788	$2
Tails of Friendship	99502	$5

Title	Book Number	Value
Taking Care of Mom (Book 2)	98880	$2
Tammy (Paper Doll)	A52	$65
Tawny Scrawny Lion and the Clever Monkey, The	128	$7
Tawny Scrawny Lion	138	$16
Tawny Scrawny Lion Saves the Day	201-58	$4
Teapot's Tale, The (Beauty and the Beast)	104-70	$2
Ten Little Animals	451	$6
That's Snow Ghost (Scooby-Doo!)	96012	$3
Things I Like	209-9	$2
Things In My House	570	$5
This Is My Body (Book 6)	96013	$2
Thomas and the Big, Big Bridge	10335	$3
Three Bears, The	82576	$3
Thumbelina (Barbie)	10452	$3
Thumper	D119	$10
Time For Bed	301-55	$5
Timid Little Kitten, The	98881	$2
Tom and Jerry	117	$14
Tom and Jerry Meet Little Quack	181	$10
Tom Thumb	353	$8
Tommy Visits the Doctor	480	$6

Title	Book Number	Value
Tommy's Wonderful Rides	63	$17
Tonka	D80	$16
Train Stamps	A26	$45
Trucks (2 Paper Model Trucks)	A6	$175
Tweety and Sylvester In Birds of a Feather	110-78	$3
Tweety's Global Patrol	110-82	$3
Twins, The	227	$75
Uncle Mistletoe	175	$27
Very Best Easter Bunny, The (Pooh)	98795	$2
Very Best Home For Me!, The (Formerly: Animal Friends)	204-25	$4
Very Busy Barbie	107-90	$3
Wagon Train	326	$18
Wait-For-Me Kitten	463	$8
We Help Daddy	468	$12
Wedding Is Beautiful, A	98877	$2
Welcome to Little Golden Book Land	209-62	$4
What Am I?	58	$14
What Am I? (Puzzle Edition)	58	$150
What Lily Goose Found	163	$6
What Will I Be?	206-3	$2
What's Next Elephant? (Formerly: The Big Elephant)	206-61	$4

Title	Book Number	Value
What's Up In the Attic?	108-58	$4
When Bunny Grows Up (Fomerly: The Bunny Book)	311-71	$3
Where Do Kisses Come From?	99503	$3
Where Is the Poky Little Puppy?	467	$8
Where's Fifi? (Minnie 'n Me)	100-77	$2
Where's Woodstock?	111-63	$4
Which Witch Is Which?	98770	$2
White Bunny and His Magic Nose, The	305	$12
Who Comes to Your House?	575	$5
Who Needs a Cat?	507	$7
Winnie-the-Pooh—A Day to Remember (Unstated First)	101-26	$10
Wonder of Easter, The	98796	$2
Wonderful School, The	582	$8
Wonders of Nature	293	$14
Woodsy Owl and the Trail Bikers	107	$7
Words	205-4	$2
Year On the Farm, A	37	$20
Zappo Change-O!	99812	$3
Zorro	D68	$16
Zorro and the Secret Plan	D77	$16